Business Letters
Made Simple

Business Letters
Made Simple

Betty and Warner Hutchinson

A MADE SIMPLE BOOK
DOUBLEDAY
NEW YORK LONDON TORONTO SYDNEY AUCKLAND

A Made Simple Book

PUBLISHED BY DOUBLEDAY

a division of Bantam Doubleday Dell Publishing Group, Inc.,
666 Fifth Avenue, New York, New York 10103

MADE SIMPLE and DOUBLEDAY are trademarks of Doubleday,
a division of Bantam Doubleday Dell Publishing Group, Inc.

Library of Congress Cataloging in Publication Data
Hutchinson, Betty.
 Business letters made simple.
 "Made simple books."
 Includes index.
 1. Commercial correspondence. I. Hutchinson,
Warner. II. Title.
HF5726.H87 1985   651.7′5   84-24717
ISBN 0-385-19427-7

Contents

Introduction

Business Letters Made Simple is an easy-to-use manual for business letter writing. It provides the following features:

1. A discussion of effective business communications.
2. Guidelines to clear business letter writing.
3. Special considerations for international business letter writing.
4. The format and elements of a business letter.
5. Types of business letters.
6. Tips on how to write each kind of business letter.
7. Examples of each kind of business letter.
8. Special features of business letter writing made possible by electronic word processing.

You will find you can easily use or adapt many letters, paragraphs, and phrases directly from *Business Letters Made Simple*. We have written the sample letters for the purpose of saving you the effort of having to "reinvent" all your own letters from scratch. By changing or adapting a word here and a phrase there, you can readily make these "standard" paragraphs yours. They will then reflect your company or business situation and your own personality.

Whenever you need to write a letter on a new topic—one that is out of the ordinary for you—there is a discussion of that kind of letter in this book and samples for you to use or adapt.

Business Letters Made Simple is the result of six decades of combined experience in writing business letters. The authors have written these letters from senior management, large international corporate experience, from middle management, middle-sized business experience, and from privately held small business experience. They have combined a breadth of subject matter, communications theory, and knowledge of electronic word processing to make *Business Letters Made Simple* a unique, contemporary, practical guide for today's business letter writers.

Business Letters
Made Simple

CHAPTER 1

The Importance of Clear Communications

Communications is the lifeline of modern business. It is essential that ideas be sent and received in a timely and clear manner. A message received too late or one that does not readily disclose its author's intent is at best, useless or, at worst, harmful.

PRINCIPLES OF EFFECTIVE COMMUNICATIONS

Before going into the format, mechanics, and contents of business letters, it is helpful to consider some basic principles from communications theory. Once these principles are grasped and adopted, you can approach any letter-writing task with confidence. You know what the letter is supposed to accomplish, what you have to do, and how your reader will interpret it. You know these things because you apply the principles of sound communications theory to your business letter writing.

The Sender and the Receiver

First, there are two *people* involved in a business letter: you and the person to whom you address the letter. In communications theory you are called the "sender"; the person to whom you address the letter is called the "receiver." There may also be some others who look over your shoulder, people to whom you send copies of the letter. These are called "observers." Their role essentially is passive, whereas the roles of the sender and the receiver are active. You are trying to get the receiver to *understand* something (cognitive response) and possibly to *do* something (active response). In some communications you are even trying to get the receiver to *feel* something (emotive response).

The Subject

Second, there is a concept or subject you have in mind. Usually, this concept is a vague cluster of ideas. It is not until you begin to express this concept in words that it starts to take a clear, identifiable form. You need to give some structure to this concept, to organize it in a logical outline, to make parts of it concrete with names and figures, to give it a kind of life of its own with a beginning and an ending. For instance, you may want to talk over some business matter with the receiver. That's your vague concept. But when it comes to actually inviting him to come to your office for a business discussion, you need to expand that concept into a specific day and hour for an appointment, an agenda for points to be discussed with any backup financial and technical data that should be included in the discussion, plus a gen- eralized impression of where you hope the discussion will lead. The actual discussion may arrive at some other conclusion, but you need to have your primary goal in mind for the meeting to be other than a social visit.

The Message

Third, there is the message you send to the receiver. This is a written replication of your subject. In your message, you want your receiver to have in his mind the same subject or concept that you have in yours. You are trying to enable him to see the concept in the same way you see it, to understand it as you understand it, to feel about it as you feel about it. The success of your business letter can be measured by the degree to which your receiver has in the end the same view of the subject that you had when you wrote the letter.

Transcultural Communications

In some instances your message will have to cross cultural lines. This may occur when you write to people within this country of a different educational experience, of a different social group, or to people of a different technical specialty. When you write to these people, you cannot take it for granted that they will readily understand your technical terms or your professional assumptions. And it most surely occurs when you write to people overseas, to people who use English as a second language, to people who have different managerial systems, to people who order their government and society by different patterns. When you write to these people, you have to take even less common ground for granted.

THE LANGUAGE OF EFFECTIVE COMMUNICATIONS

Range of Sending and Receiving

Every user of a language is both a sender and a receiver. You normally understand many more words that you hear or read than you normally use in your own speech or writing. You recognize them or guess their meaning close enough, even though you may not use them as a working word in your own everyday vocabulary. This is true also of grammatical forms. You have a feeling for when grammar is correct and when it is less formal, even though you may have forgotten all the special names for verb forms or all the rules for dealing with gerunds. Usually we are more at home with our spoken language than with our written language. Our reading and listening vocabularies are considerably larger than are our writing and speaking vocabularies.

Levels of Formality

We use our language at different levels of formality. A person who is speaking to the annual meeting of a company's stockholders uses a different level of vocabulary and grammar than the same person does when telling a joke at a backyard barbecue. A person who is interviewing for a job uses a different level of formal language than does the same person when describing the interview to a close friend.

Levels of Education

There is educated language, that is, language used in formal and informal situations by a person who has had years of formal education. A college professor who gives a lecture to a scholarly organization uses educated formal language; and when he tells friends about his vacation, he uses educated informal language. In his lecture he will use technical and literary words that he may not normally use when talking about his vacation. This high-level educated language—doctors talking to each other about medicine, lawyers talking to each other about a legal case, computer scientists talking to each other about high-technology developments— includes many technical words that give accuracy to language and serve as abbreviations in rapid communication between specialists, but these words are usually unintelligible to those who are outside the specialty.

There is also uneducated language, the language of people who have limited formal education. This language might be street language in a big city or mountain language in a rural hill community. The people who use uneducated language are not ignorant, indeed they may be quite brilliant, but their language is not the product of formal education. It is the product of the living environment. This language, too, has many technical words that make the speech colorful, but also make it unintelligible to those who are outsiders.

Levels for Business Correspondence

Most of your business correspondence is in the common (that is, shared by both educated and uneducated users) area of the language. This guarantees the greatest degree of communication—it is not so educated or formal that most people fail to understand it, nor is it so slangy and informal that people feel it is unimportant or reject it as inappropriate. However, if you write about a technical subject in your business letter, you will probably use special words that "insiders" know, and these words are generally not in the common area of the language. In this kind of letter, parts of the letter will be in the *technical* business correspondence level of the language.

STEPS IN EFFECTIVE COMMUNICATIONS

There are some standard steps to take to achieve clear communications with your receiver.

Make Sure You Clarify the Subject to Yourself

If you have not clarified the subject to yourself, you will never be able to communicate it to the receiver. The first step is to satisfy yourself that you fully understand what you want to say, then work to find the clearest words in which to express the concept. We say "work" because sometimes you will have to try two or three times before you are satisfied that you have the best possible wording. For this reason drafts are essential for important letters.

Make Sure You Understand the Receiver As Much As Possible

The second step is to try to put yourself in the place of the receiver. What can you presuppose he knows that the two of you share in common? What will you have to define further or to expand upon? What will move him to take the action you want him to take or to feel the response you want him to feel? What is his "need to know" in order for him to enter into your concept? The more you have worked with the receiver in the past, the less you will have to elaborate your concept, since you and he have already learned to think along the same lines. The less you have worked with your receiver, the more explicit you will have to be in your message to ensure that your concept is adequately conveyed.

Analyze the Nature of Your Message

Much also depends on the nature of your message. A letter requesting payment of an overdue bill can be much shorter and to the point (since you both know about the history of the transaction) than does a proposal for developing a new software product for a computer products company. A letter of enquiry will be less formally worked out than a complete business pro-posal.

Determine the Response You Want to Elicit

Much depends on the type of response you wish to elicit in your receiver. Do you want understanding only or understanding and action? How much emotion do you need to generate in order to set in motion the action you want your reader to take? If you are writing a sales letter or a fund-raising letter, the action you call for (a purchase or a contribution) should serve to satisfy some need your reader senses (a new gadget to make barbecuing easier) or to make him feel good about himself in some way (helping a child in a Third World orphanage). Some words are emotion-filled: "the joy of helping to feed hungry children and to give them hope"; "this new wonder of modern chemistry will restore that showroom sheen to your car, and heads will turn to watch you as you drive by in the sparkling sunlight." The emotion in a covering letter with a contract, in contrast, is much more subdued: "I take great pleasure in sending you this signed contract. After long hours of mutual preparation and negotiation, we are delighted to take this first formal step in what we hope will be a long business journey together."

ELEMENTS IN EFFECTIVE COMMUNICATIONS

There are some elements that are a necessary part of effective communications. Every busi-ness letter will have these elements to some degree.

Clarity

You know your subject well and have thought it out clearly. You choose the best possible way of expressing your subject. You keep the receiver foremost in mind, since your intent in sending the communication is to enable him to share your perspective on the subject. Care in thinking, care in choosing words, and care in evaluating how best to convey your message to the receiver results in clarity. A breakdown at any one of these points leads to a muddled communication. You may be clear to yourself, but that in itself is of little avail in achieving effective business communications.

Accuracy

You need to make sure you have your facts right. Most business letters contain references to dates, money, events, products, processes, schedules, agreements, relationships, and the like. You are building on past fact to move matters forward in some way. If you present your facts loosely or inaccurately, you contribute to confused communication. You show the receiver that you are careless about the facts, encouraging him to have less regard for you or to be equally indifferent to the facts. Double-check your facts for the sake of the business arrangement as well as for your own professional reputation.

Brevity

Be as brief as possible. That may mean a one-paragraph letter or a ten-page letter. The best length depends on the nature of the message. If you dictate your letters on a dictating machine or to a stenographer, your tendency will be to think aloud as you dictate and therefore to be far more wordy than is necessary. Discipline yourself to go over draft copies of dictated correspondence and to remove unnecessary word clutter. If you do this regularly, you will begin to condition yourself to avoid introducing such word clutter into your dictation. When you dictate, it takes concentration to avoid using verbal filler during those moments you are searching for the next thought.

Your receiver—like you—leads a busy work life. There is never enough time to do everything that should be done, much less everything that could be done. Reading correspondence is a time-consuming interruption from other essential tasks. Therefore, make it easier for your receiver by keeping your message to one page if at all possible. Put your main point up front. Organize each paragraph so your concept is readily understood. Make your desired action clear and separate from your general discussion. And do all this with a few, well-chosen words.

Timeliness

Make sure your letter arrives in time for your receiver to act before it is too late. He needs time just to get to your letter. He may be away on a business trip, even a vacation. He may have an emergency in his own business that occupies him for a day or so. Do not take it for granted that he will look at your letter and give it his full attention the moment it arrives.

He will also need time to consider your letter's message. He may have to have further study or research done by his staff before he can respond. He may have to consult with an accountant, a colleague, a professional adviser, or his boss before he can begin to fashion a response. He may have to send your letter around to others and call a committee together to consider it. In other words, gauge your expectations of response—and therefore your timing—realistically by the importance to the receiver of your message. And remember, he may put quite a different set of values on your message than you do. You may think it vital to your business, whereas it is merely routine to your reader.

A Record

Your business letter serves as a record of discussion and agreements with your receiver. Word your letter in such a way that it includes an accurate and adequate summary of what was said and agreed to. It may also serve as a record of your suggestions, requests, or demurrals. Keep in mind as you write the letter that someday you or your successor will pull the letter from the file to look for key information relating to business arrangements with the receiver. If the record of relationships cannot be clearly traced in the correspondence, important information may be lost, to the detriment of your company's business.

When documents are sent, a covering letter should go with the documents, naming them. This covering letter serves as a record that the documents were indeed sent and when.

One of the most frequent requests made by an executive is "Bring me the file." When you receive a letter from someone with whom you have had previous dealing—whether long-term or brief—you need the file to refresh your memory on how this newly received letter fits in with the relationship to date. As you answer the letter, you may also refer to the file to know what you and the other person have said about the matter in the past. In your reply, you carry the discussion forward another step. Your file is an ongoing record of the steps you and the other person have taken together to date. The letter you write should be written with the file in mind, since you will undoubtedly refer to it again in the future.

Personal

There was a time when business correspondence was kept as impersonal as possible. This resulted in convoluted, often stuffy, circumlocutions to avoid any personal reference. Such phrases as "it is requested that . . . ," "it has been brought to our attention that . . . ," and "it is expected that . . ." were hallmarks of good business practice. This approach resulted in extra verbiage, weak language, and unclear communications.

Today's business letter is far more personal and direct. You refer to yourself as "I" instead of the company "we" if you are really talking about your own opinion or decision. You refer to the receiver as "you." The tone is generally one of a friendly conversation, such as you would have over lunch when talking about the subject.

Often you may write a personal closing paragraph in which you ask about family or vacation or some commonly enjoyed pastime. The purpose of this last, personal paragraph is to assure the receiver that you are continuing to maintain a friendly relationship with him throughout the more formal business dealings contained in the body of the letter. This assures you both that when you next see each other, talk with each other on the telephone, or write to each other, you are both proceeding from a shared feeling of friendship and personal regard for each other as well as from a shared business interest. This is quite the opposite of approaching each other only formally or even as antagonists in a conflict or possible conflict setting.

This personal paragraph in a letter serves much the same purpose as the short comments about weather or family or health that you make on the telephone before you get into the actual business part of your call, or the personal chitchat you have for a minute or two before getting down to business when you meet in his office or yours.

EFFECTIVE COMMUNICATIONS WITH OVERSEAS BUSINESS CORRESPONDENTS

If your overseas correspondent learned English as a second language, his English may tend to be schoolbookish, since it is a language he learned at school. He will tend to apply strict dictionary meanings to words and will most often use the primary or major dictionary definition. He will also tend to use grammar in a precise, but not always accurate or idiomatic, way. In fact, sometimes you may even have the feeling that a schoolchild is writing. Don't be misled by this; this correspondent may be brilliant in his field and gifted in his own language, even though he is limited to a schoolchild's range of vocabulary and grammar in English. He needs to be understood at the level of his professional and business competence, and not thought less of because his English usage is somewhat limited. His window into the range of English is smaller than that of a native English user. Since English is such a widely used international language for science and business, his proficiency in his own specialized area is probably greater than his proficiency in informal, idiomatic English. Of course, the more exposure he has to English the larger his "window" will be.

From Romance Language Areas

If your correspondent's native language is a Romance language (Spanish, French, Italian, or Portuguese—languages that developed from Latin), it is necessary to stay alert to possible misunderstandings that can arise due to the fact that many English words are based on Latin roots. But even though they share the same Latin original, the words developed differently in English and in Spanish or French. For instance, your Spanish correspondent when writing in English may speak of the "rentability" of a new product. A native English user will first think of the suitability of leasing the product or renting it out. However, your correspondent bases "rentability" on the root term *renta*, which means "income in general" or "profit," so the meaning he has in mind when he uses "rentability" is expressed in English by "profitability." (Incidentally, the English word "rent" came from the Old French word *rente*, which meant "income from property"—a restricted meaning that has remained pretty much unchanged in English; whereas in French the word "rente" has expanded to include the concepts of "income," "dividends," and "interest," as well as "profit.")

Sometimes words have such different ranges of meaning that they can be misleading. In Spanish the word *profesor* refers to any teacher—whether a kindergarten teacher or the holder of an elite university chair. In English the word "professor" is used only of university or college teachers, except when it is used colloquially to refer to a person of some unusual skill, such as a ragtime piano player. You may get quite the wrong meaning from your correspondent's letter if you automatically assume he uses the word in the English sense.

An example often encountered is the use of the word "rationalize." In American English this usually means to "explain away" or to "justify to oneself." But a Spanish-language user (or even a British English user) bases his use of the word on the root meaning "rational" in the sense of to "think about," so he means to "make organized and logical sense of something and put matters into a logical and coherent framework." When he wants to "rationalize" an organization, he wants to restructure it according to a logical analysis. You can readily see how an American and his overseas correspondent can become confused by getting quite different meanings from the same word.

Technical Words

Highly technical words, however, are generally clear to both parties, since they share a common international scientific and professional vocabulary. Every accountant means the same thing when he or she speaks of a "credit" or a "debit"; and every physiologist means the same thing by "enzymes" or "hormones."

Your awareness of these characteristics of cross-cultural communication will help you grasp the content of overseas correspondence more accurately. If you have regular correspondence with people in a foreign country—even though the correspondence takes place in English—you should have a bilingual dictionary at hand. Whenever you see an expression that looks more or less normal but doesn't really make good sense, look up key words in the dictionary. You'll usually find that one of the possible definitions makes good sense, even though the meaning that first comes to mind from the appearance of the word(s) does not do so.

When writing to overseas people for whom English is a second language, use the same "window" of moderately formal, dictionary-definition English that they normally use. And use the first and obvious definition of the word rather than the literary or figurative meanings of the word. Better straightforward clarity than a more subtle use of the language that may only befuddle your reader. Above all, avoid everyday American slang or colloquial language. A Pakistani correspondent, for instance, knows the meaning of "hot" and of "dog." But unless he has lived in America, he probably doesn't know what a "hot dog" (something to eat) is. And he almost surely doesn't know the meaning of "Hot dog!" (an expression of great joy or enthusiasm), nor does he describe a person with a showy style of skateboarding or skiing as a "hot dog."

British English

If your correspondent is a native British English user—whether from England, Nigeria, India, Singapore, or New Zealand—cross-cultural communication is generally easier, but it still is not to be taken for granted. In formal, dictionary definitions of many everyday words, there can be confusing differences. British "corn" is American "wheat"; American "corn" is British "maize." British "tin" is American "can" (of vegetables); American "thread" is British "cotton" (for sewing). British "bonnet" is American "hood" (of automobile [British "motor car"]); American "trunk" is British "boot" (in the same automobile); but American "trunk" is also British "portmanteau" (a large, hinged container for packing clothes when traveling).

When slang or informal idiom is used, the differences of meaning between Americans and British English increase considerably. This is one reason why Americans seldom laugh at British jokes (and the other way around), because jokes are usually a play on words at the informal level. When the meaning of the words has to be explained, the suddenness of the unexpected insight (the cause of the humorous reaction) is lost. A joke that has to be explained is no longer funny.

George Bernard Shaw once quipped that Americans and the English were separated by the same language. This witticism contains enough truth to give warning that business correspondence between American English and British English users conveys the greatest degree of mutual comprehension when it is conducted in a kind of "mid-Atlantic" English. This is a standard, direct, nonidiomatic language that avoids regional color or the latest fad in words.

A Sample Letter

Sample 1 is an example of a business letter to an overseas correspondent.

Sample 1. Letter to an Overseas Correspondent

ABC COMPANY, INC.
123 MAIN STREET
CENTERVILLE, IL 66666

February 15, 1995

Sr. Pedro Carcamo-Gonzales
ABC International, S.A.
Apto. 456
123 Avenida del Norte
San Jose, Costa Rica

Dear Sr. Carcamo:

I received your letter of January 3, 1995. In your letter you ask about purchasing software for use in your accounting department.

Our company has an excellent software program for accounting, inventory control, and payroll. Although we developed this software for use on the Zenox Business Microcomputer, we also have versions for use on other popular microcomputers. In your letter you did not tell us which microcomputer you use. Please tell me the name of the manufacturer, the model number, and the memory capacity (number of bytes) of your microcomputer, and I will send you complete information about the proper software program for your needs.

I look forward to hearing from you soon.

With every good wish, I remain

Yours sincerely,

John P. Wizard
International Services

JPW/amc

The following characteristics should be noted:

DATE: Most overseas correspondents use a day-month-year sequence when using only figures. Thus, "12/2/95" is "February 12, 1995," not "December 2, 1995," for most overseas people. Avoid possible confusion by spelling out the month.

COMPLIMENTARY TITLE: Although you can use "Mr." in addressing overseas correspondents, it is more courteous to use the appropriate title in their own language. In this case, "Sr." stands for "Señor." You could use, "Herr" (German), "M." (French, abbreviation for "Monsieur"), and so on.

NAME: Use the proper form of the person's name. In the name of a man from a Spanish-speaking country, the man's mother's family name is part of his formal name. His father's family name is first, and his mother's family name is joined to it by a hyphen. However, when he is addressed directly, only the father's family name is used. Legally and formally he is "Carcamo (father's family name)-Gonzales (mother's family name)," but when spoken to directly he is "Sr. Carcamo." A married woman's formal and legal name is made up by joining her father's family name and her husband's family name with "y" ("and"), but she is addressed by her husband's name. Thus, "Sra. Teresa Lopez y Carcamo" would be addressed directly as "Sra. Carcamo." Other languages have other conventions. By using them correctly, you show that you care about the person and the traditions of his culture. He may be sensitive enough to note with pleasure that you have been polite and correct if you use his name properly, and he will be sure to notice when you use his name improperly. At best, he will smile at your ignorance, and at worst, he may take offense at your carelessness.

BOX NUMBER: In some languages the word for "Post Office Box" may remind you of some other meaning in English. In Spanish the word is *"Apartado"* or *"Apto."* It is not an "apartment." Because the post office personnel in the correspondent's country may not readily understand English, use an address form taken from your correspondent's letterhead to make sure your letter arrives without unnecessary delay.

BODY OF LETTER: Express yourself in clear, direct form. Avoid passives, perfects, and pluperfects as much as possible. Use the present tense, simple past tense, and simple future tense, but avoid conditional future tense forms whenever possible. Think of your correspondent as an intelligent person, but one who has a limited command of idiomatic English. Brand names and technical language, however, do not pose any great problem.

CLOSING: Overseas correspondents tend to be a bit more flowery than American business letter writers. Therefore, the extra expression of good wishes and personal reference is appropriate. Latin American correspondents normally convey their greetings to their reader's family if the family is known to them.

CHAPTER 2
Format of a Business Letter

GENERAL

The format of a business letter is its physical shape, its layout and design. Clarity and simplicity are the key design elements. Clarity means making the contents of a letter clear to the reader from its appearance as well as its words. Lack of clutter and busyness enable the reader to focus on the main point of the letter quickly and accurately. Fussiness and overcrowdedness distract the reader's eye, confusing the important with what merely fills space.

Reduce Keystrokes

The rule that governs today's business letter format almost more than any other is the "reduce the keystrokes" rule. Every keystroke takes time, costs money, and introduces the possibility of making an error that will only have to be corrected later. Business letters that take the fewest keystrokes to write are less expensive than letters that say the same thing but take twenty-five or fifty additional keystrokes to type or to word process. With word processor operators being paid high wages, every fifty keystrokes saved is a valuable cost reduction to the company. Simplicity, therefore, means a letter that is the result of the least necessary number of keystrokes.

Block Left

Business letters are increasingly entirely "flush left" or "block left." All the lines begin at the left-hand typing margin, with no indentations at all. There are no tabs for paragraph indents, for date indents, or for signature/title indents.

Each tab that is used takes one or more keystrokes. So tabs have been eliminated from most business correspondence. In this book we will show alternative formats with indentations, but we will normally use the block left format in our examples (just as we do in our own business correspondence).

One Page

As much as possible, a business letter is written to fit on one page. The reason for this is that executives have little time to pore over long, complex letters. They prefer their information in condensed, concise, concentrated form—in a format as easy to read as possible. They glance through stacks of papers daily to glean what they need to know in the midst of committee-filled, appointment-filled, telephone-filled, deadline-filled days. You need only imagine yourself in the place of the person who receives your letter to see the value of your writing to the point. Just as most appointments ought not take over thirty minutes, so most letters ought not take over a page.

And just as there are the occasional appointments that need to be longer, but therefore need summary points from time to time to keep them in sharp focus, so some letters may have to take up more than one page. But in these letters a sharper outline with a final summary paragraph are essential to keep the reader from losing the point you are making. For the longer letter, paragraphs may be numbered; summary sentences or paragraphs may be indented to draw attention to them.

FORMAT FOR A SINGLE-PAGE LETTER

A business letter generally consists of date, address, salutation, body, complimentary closing, and signature/title. It may include a subject or reference line.

Date

The date is normally typed in a month-day-year sequence. The month should be spelled out in full; avoid abbreviations or numbers only. The date, then, should be expressed as "March 24, 1992"; not "Mar. 24, 1992" or "3/24/92." A comma separates the day from the year.

Some businesses are, however, adopting a date system that has long been followed in military correspondence. This is the day-month-year sequence. No punctuation is used in this sequence: "24 March 1992" is the accepted use of the day-month-year date. This sequence saves one keystroke. It is a system that is widely used in Europe, and so it is suitable to use in international correspondence.

When the Europeans convert this day-month-year sequence to a numeric equivalent, they show "24 March 1992" as "24/3/92." This equivalent can become confusing to North Americans if the first two numbers are 12 or less. Is "11/5/90" "November 5, 1990" or "11 May 1990?" You need to have clear signals with your European correspondent to make sure that numerically expressed dates are not misread. You might want to make a note on the letter when you receive it so it can be referred to correctly later.

Because computers sort by numeric order, government agencies and a few businesses have adopted the year-month-day sequence for internal use, with all numbers expressed in two digits. In this sequence, "24 March 1992" is rendered "920324." Thus, any date prior to 24 March 1992 would be a lesser number than 920324; and any date after would be a larger number. The computer can deal easily with that kind of sequencing. Even though it is entirely possible for computer programmers to allow you to date correspondence and reports normally and to program the computer to do the resequencing to a strictly numerical order, some data-processing departments have taken the easier road of making people adjust to the computer. So far, most uses of the year-month-day sequence are limited to highly specialized forms and reports, and do not as yet affect general business correspondence.

People in the business world readily understand either "March 24, 1992," or "24 March 1992." Choose one for your standard use and be consistent in its use in all your correspondence.

The date line is the first line in the letter. It is placed two or three lines below your letterhead and flush left:

March 24, 1992

Address

The address usually consists of the name of the person to whom the letter is sent, often with a social title and his company title, the name of the firm, and the mailing address of the firm. Having a full address is good business for two reasons: It shows courtesy to the person to whom you send the letter, and it contains a full record for your files of who the person is.

This latter reason may become important when you are no longer in the job position you held when you wrote the letter and your successor wonders who "John Smith" is; it is helpful at that moment if your file copy of the letter also includes the information that John Smith was "International Marketing Manager" at the time you wrote the letter.

SOCIAL OR PROFESSIONAL TITLE. You may—or may not—use a social title in the address block. Once it was required; now it is optional. A social title is "Mr.," "Mrs.," "Ms," "Miss," "Dr.," "The Hon.," or "The Rev." Since there are several keystrokes involved, and there is always the chance of choosing the wrong social title, many business letter writers just use the person's name in the address.

If a woman's social title is used, additional care is needed to choose the correct one. A married woman may choose to keep her maiden name or to use it in business. Therefore, "Mrs. Jones" socially may still be "Miss Smith" in business. Or a divorced woman may continue to use her married name ("Mrs. Wilson"); or she may revert to her unmarried name ("Miss Johnson"). Or a woman—single, married, divorced, or widowed—may choose to be addressed in correspondence as "Ms" in order to avoid any marriage-related stereotype. When you are not sure how a woman prefers to be addressed, "Ms" is the social title least open to error.

Since the social title "Ms" is not an abbreviation, it follows the pattern of "Miss" in being used without a period. "Mrs." is an abbreviation for "Mistress," a word that is no longer used in full when addressing a married woman by her surname. Even the current pronunciation of "Mrs." no longer reflects the origin of the word. "Mr." is an abbreviation of "Mister," a term of address still in common use of a man, regardless of his marital status. But keep in mind that "Miss" and "Ms" are words in their own right, not abbreviations.

If you have regular business correspondence with people in a church environment, spend some time to learn the correct social titles for men and women. The correct use of these titles are important to those who hold the titles. They will forgive outsiders who are ignorant of the fine shades of usage, but they will warm to those who have taken the trouble to seek out the "proper" form. We use the word "proper" in quotes, since each denomination and church body has its own special titles, abbreviations, and complimentary forms. Although there are Methodist bishops, Lutheran bishops, Episcopalian bishops, Roman Catholic bishops, and Orthodox bishops, each of those "brands" of bishops has a different social title. So from the point of view of letter writing, a bishop is not just a bishop. You need to know the bishop's denomination and rank in order to know the right title to use. Unless you do so much business with the leaders in a particular denomination that you have learned the protocol for that group, the best way to be sure you have the right official title and social title is to call the person's secretary and ask how the person is to be addressed.

The same is true of university positions. One university's "president" may be another's "chancellor"; one university's "dean" may be another's "provost." Here it is best to follow the lead on the person's letterhead or to call the person's secretary to ensure that you use the correct titles.

If you write regularly to military personnel, follow the patterns for that particular military service. The Navy abbreviates "Captain" as "CAPT"; the Army as "Cpt." And a Navy captain is not flattered to be mistaken for an Army captain. Each service has its own correspondence style, expressed in readily available official correspondence manuals. Get a copy from each of the services and use the titles in the fashion used by the service involved.

In a rank-conscious organization—whether the military, the university, or the church—your use of correct titles will be appreciated.

Two groups of professional people normally do not use a social title *before* their name in formal business address. A lawyer often uses "Esq." after the full name: John J. James, Esq. (In some sections of the country, a lawyer may use the form "Atty. John J. James"; in that case, "Esq." is not used.) A medical doctor uses "M.D." after the full name: Mary P. Pearson, M.D. "Mr." or "Mrs." or "Dr." is not used in these formal addresses to either lawyers or medical doctors.

Note that there is no space between the letters in "M.D." The social title "Dr." and the formal recognition of medical qualification ("M.D.") is used whether the person is a man or a woman. Medical doctors were not always held in high regard; the days of quackery are not far gone. University-level and hospital-focused medical training is less than two centuries old; so formal medical degrees are a relatively new phenomenon. To distance themselves from untrained quacks, physicians and surgeons who had formal medical degrees and certification established the protocol of using the degree after their name. "M.D." has almost become a part of the person's surname, to an extent that academic degrees in general have not. Certainly, "M.D." is an integral part of the name line in addressing a business letter to a medical doctor.

In the United States the social title "Esq." is most often a term of mutual respect given by lawyers to each other, and sometimes by nonlawyers when writing to lawyers. Women lawyers are never "Esq."; the term is reserved for males.

In Great Britain and the Commonwealth, "Esq." is sometimes used in correspondence when you want to show respect to a man (not a lawyer) but you do not know a specific honorific to use. It is a way of being extremely courteous to someone in an important position, saying, in effect, "I don't know whether you have an important title or not, but to me you are more than just a 'Mister,' you're an 'Esquire'—'an important person.'" This honorific is based on the medieval use of the term "esquire" to refer to a man who was preparing to be a knight; it was a term used of one who had formally entered the first stage of nobility. It has lost that meaning in general use, and it is now only a somewhat archaic term of formal courtesy.

BUSINESS TITLE. Use of the company or business title is optional. It is courteous and it can often be helpful later in identifying the position of the person to whom the letter was sent. Much depends on the character of the person to whom you are writing. Some (fortunately few) executives love to flaunt all the appurtenances of their office, including their title. If the title is not used, they feel abused and your business relation may suffer because their vanity is wounded. If you know you are writing to this kind of person—and you want or need to do continued business with him—use of his title in your address line furthers good business relations.

If you are writing to someone you do not know personally, use of the title is not only safe, it also ensures that the person realizes you are writing to the office represented by the title. This can be especially important when writing to the president of a company with a proposal or a complaint. In such a case, you are addressing a position in the company more than an individual.

If you are writing to a person who is more informal—one who wears his laurels lightly—he may prefer his title to be left off correspondence. This is especially true as your relationship progresses, becomes more personal, and your correspondence increases. And it is even more true if your own title is equal to or superior to his: You then relate as peers instead of positions.

The business title usually follows the person's surname. A comma is used and the title is capitalized. Parts of the title are spelled out in full. If the title is too long to fit readily on the same line as the name, the title is placed on the line just below the name:

Mr. John P. Rogers, President
Mary Lou Endicott, Assistant Marketing Director
Philip H. Conwell, M.D., Director of Aural Services
The Rt. Rev. Max Drummond, Bishop of Nelson
Maj. Gen. Roscoe X. Kelley, U.S.M.C.
Director of Logistics Services

COMPANY NAME. Either the full name of the company or its official abbreviation may be used. You may write to "International Business Machines Corporation" or "IBM Corporation." It is always safe to follow the pattern in the company's own letterhead.

You may abbreviate parts of a company name, such as "Inc.," "Co.," and "Corp." Usually, "Incorporated" is abbreviated to "Inc." Follow the company's own practice regarding "Company" and "Corporation." But even then, you may find the company itself is inconsistent in its own practice. If so, save keystrokes and abbreviate.

STREET/BOX NUMBER. The street address should include the number, street name, quadrant (if any), and street title. If the quadrant is used, it is increasingly used without periods. The street title is normally spelled out in full, although "Boulevard" is often abbreviated to "Blvd." Thus:

15307 Sunrise Highway, SW
1508 K Street, NE

If a post office box is used, the United States Postal Service prefers that you use "Post Office Box" or "POB" instead of just "Box." This is to differentiate *their* box from a company's internal sorting box. "POB" is easier to type than the other two, although "Box" is still the most generally used.

Postal Service instructions point out that if you use *both* the street address and a POB address, the one on the line just above the city name is the one that will be used. Thus, if you address the envelope:

ABC Company
123 Third Avenue
POB 456
Anywhere, MN 77777

the envelope will be delivered to the post office box, not the Third Avenue address. Reverse the two lines:

ABC Company
POB 456
123 Third Avenue
Anywhere, MN 77777

and the envelope would then be delivered to the street address. This Postal Service instruction, however, is more often ignored than followed by the Postal Service locally; they tend to deal with a company's mail in bulk, whether it is addressed to the one or the other.

The main exception to bulk handling of company mail is when the company uses the Postal Service for presorting mail by the use of several post office boxes. A company may measure direct mail sales efforts by having responses from certain promotional campaigns, space ads, or mailings come to specific boxes; or a company may use a specific box number on pread-dressed envelopes that are sent out with monthly billings in order to control the security of funds. When you write a business letter to a company executive, however, you normally use the company's main address, not a direct-mail-related or billing-receipt-related box number.

CITY, STATE, ZIP. The last line of the address is the city-state-ZIP line. Use the Postal Service abbreviation for the state. These abbreviations are two-letter, no-punctuation abbreviations. "NY" is much simpler to type than is "N. Y." "MA" is much simpler than "'Mass." In Postal Service Service Centers that use optical scanners for mail sorting, the typed, two-letter abbreviation is much more accurately read by the scanner than is the name of the state spelled out in full or traditionally abbreviated ("Calif.," "Colo.," "Mich.," "Wisc.," etc.). Use of the Postal Service-approved abbreviations may speed your letter to its destination. "CT" does indeed look less elegant than "Connecticut," so if you still want to use "Connecticut," use it in the letter itself, but use "CT" on the envelope.

Always use the ZIP Code. The Postal Service sells an annual ZIP code listing, the *National Five Digit ZIP Code and Post Office Directory,* which gives all the ZIP Codes in the United States and its possessions. This book includes the street and house/business numbers for all communities that have more than one ZIP Code for the community.

Increasingly, businesses are using the "ZIP + 4" extended code. The final four numbers in this code identify the actual carrier route and delivery sequence, in addition to the standard ZIP Code's identification of the postal region and specific post office. Use of this code gives the business preferential postal rates for its bulk First-Class mailings, such as monthly billings. ZIP + 4 will more and more come into usage, so include it in your address line for those companies that adopt its use.

Subject Line

Occasionally, you may wish to highlight the subject matter of your letter by writing a subject line. The subject itself is often preceded by "Re:" or "Subj:" in order to make it clear that you are writing about that particular subject. It is not necessary to type the subject line in capital letters or to underline it. The fact that you have placed it at the head of your letter gives it adequate emphasis. Usually, the subject line is a line space below the date and a line space above the salutation:

March 24, 1992

Re: Overdue Tables for Your Article

Dear Mr. James:

We are now preparing the final copy for the 1992 Annual Review of Artificial Intelligence, and we find that you have not yet provided us with the tables you have indicated are to be used in your article. Could you please get these tables to us before Friday, April 15.

Salutation

The salutation is the line in which you directly address the person to whom you are writing. Normally, "Dear" is the first word; this is followed by the person's name.

FIRST NAME. *We* prefer using the first (given) name only with people we know or have done business with over a period of time. Nonetheless, we are increasingly getting business mail from complete strangers who address us as "Dear Betty" or "Dear Warner," just as we often have young voices on the telephone, even at such prestigious firms as IBM, thanking us for our order with a cheery "Thanks for your order, Warner, and call on us again soon." Although we recognize the trend toward more informal business dealings, we still would rather *invite* people to call us by our first names if we have any choice in the matter. Or at the very least we like to have the practice evolve out of an ongoing relationship with some participation on our part. So you can understand that our recommendation is to err on the side of decorum.

Once the other person uses your first name, feel free to use his first name in return. Not to do so is to remain in a subordinate role unnecessarily, or to suggest a level of distance in your relationship that may be offensive and may mar your business dealings. "First naming" in business correspondence is a matter of delicate etiquette; advancing to a first-name basis marks a step into new business relationships.

SOCIAL OR PROFESSIONAL TITLE. Use a social or professional title if you do not use the first name. Even though you addressed the letter to "John J. James," you would now say "Dear Mr. James." This would also apply if you addressed the letter to "John J. James, Esq." or to "The Rev. John J. James." "John J. James, M.D." becomes "Dear Dr. James." Even though "The Rev. John J. James" becomes "Dear Mr. James," "The Rt. Rev. John J. James" becomes "Dear Bishop James." "The Hon. John J. James" becomes "Dear Senator James" or "Dear Congressman James" or "Dear Judge James" or "Dear Alderman James," depending on the position or role that is the reason for the honorific.

"Mr.," "Mrs.," or "Dr." are never spelled out when used with a person's surname. Titles of position are sometimes abbreviated when used with a person's surname but are more courteous when spelled out: "Dear Professor James" is better than "Dear Prof. James"; "Dear Senator James" is better than "Dear Sen. James"; "Dear Admiral James" is better than "Dear Adm. James"; and so on.

The salutation in a business letter is normally followed by a colon. "Dear Mr. James:" is the standard form.

If you are writing a very formal letter, you may use "My dear Mr. James" but this level of usage is fading. It is mostly used with church dignitaries, as in "My dear Bishop James."

A salutation to a business rather than to an individual is awkward, though sometimes necessary. "Dear Sir" is proper, but sometimes seems sexist. "Dear ABC Company" is satisfactory, though impersonal. "Dear Friends" or "Dear Colleagues" seems out of place. Since most "Dear Friend" salutations introduce either fund-raising letters or sales pitches, you tend to lower your letter to that level when you use that salutation. "Dear Sir/Madam" is archaic and stilted. We use "Dear ABC Company" if we have to, but more often we will go to the expense of calling the company to learn the name of the proper person to address the letter to in order to make the letter more personal. Such a letter also tends to get closer attention, since it is always more effective to write to an individual in a company—who then *has* to do something with the correspondence—than to write merely to the company-at-large and let a clerk in the mailroom decide who should handle this correspondence.

Body

The body of the letter contains your message. You need to tell your reader what you want him to know or do. And you need to introduce the letter by reference to whatever has gone on before or to what is the cause for the letter's being written. You need to give any background or special data that will enable your reader to take the right action or to understand more fully what you want him to know. And you need to close with a final summary or an indication of your willingness to help your reader at the next step. If you know your reader well, you may wish to close with a more personal note, thus assuring the reader that you continue to have a friendly interest in him as well as business interest.

In a sense, you should tell your reader what you are going to say, then say it, and then tell him what you have said. Another way of putting it: You prepare the reader for your message; you deliver it; and then you suggest the next step, now that the message has been delivered.

The first paragraph in the body of the letter should contain enough of the background for the reader to call the subject matter to mind or to direct him to the right files if he needs the previous correspondence before him. The two sample first paragraphs that follow illustrate this:

This is further to our telephone conversation of July 17, in which we discussed the quality control procedures needed in manufacturing the new Mark II clamps. You said you wanted the results of our quality control tests of the past six months.

Thank you for your letter of August 12, in which you indicate that you have not yet received your order of windscreens, and in which you stress your urgent need to stock these windscreens at the beginning of the summer season.

These two sample first paragraphs tell the reader what the subject matter is for the rest of the letter that follows. And they refer the reader to any previous contact—whether orders, letters, telephone calls, meetings, or personal conversations. This enables him to place the letter in its right setting. The paragraph also summarizes for the reader what you understand to be the crux of the matter to be considered. It shows him you really do understand what his concern is, or it may alert him to the fact that you have not really understood his primary concern. If he sees that you have missed his main point, he now knows that he has to restate it to you in a way that will make it clear.

The main purpose of the opening paragraph is to set the stage for the main part of the discussion. It introduces the ''characters''—the items to be discussed—and notes their circumstances at the present time. This paragraph ensures that both you and your reader are viewing the same matter from essentially the same perspective.

Sometimes there is no past relationship. Your opening paragraph then must serve both as an introduction and as a foreword to the body of your letter:

This is to invite your consideration of a new service we at ABC Company have tailored for "white table cloth" restaurants like yours. This service is a computer-assisted record-keeping system that gives you complete control of your bar and food inventory with no added time or cost to you.

Don James at the Tutti Frutti Restaurant suggested that I write you about our computer-assisted record-keeping system for "white table cloth" restaurants. We've given Don better control of his bar and food inventory at no additional time or cost to him. And he thought you would be interested in hearing how we can do the same for you.

The first sample above is a ''cold'' opener; you have no previous contact with the reader, nor do you know of any intermediary. It is less likely to get the careful reading that the second sample will probably enjoy. Here the opening paragraph immediately calls on the good will of a mutual acquaintance, even though the reader himself does not personally know you. In this sample his response to your letter will be partly based on what he thinks of Don James.

The key in wording a cold opener is to appeal to the reader's interests and experience. He does not really want to learn about you and your company. He wants to run his own company or department better, and so will have an interest in yours only as you can convince him that you can help him accomplish his purposes more effectively.

Most cold opener letters are sales letters of some kind. You want to sell your services or product to another company or to individual consumers. And yet you do not want your letter to sound just like a direct mail sales pitch, since you are going to the trouble of writing a personal, thoughtful letter. Your first problem is to get the reader beyond the first paragraph into the rest of the letter. To do this, you must appeal to some interest he has that will be served by what you have to offer. When you finish writing the first paragraph of such a letter to John Smith, ask yourself, ''If I were Smith, why would I want to read this any further?''

The other kinds of cold openers are an announcement or a threat. The announcement is usually a pleasure:

It gives me great pleasure to inform you that you have been selected to membership in the XYZ Society.

Sometimes the announcement is less pleasurable:

We regret to inform you that your 1988 XXX automobile is subject to recall for the installation of a new braking system.

The threat usually relates to credit and collections or to legal action. The formulas most often used in these kinds of letters are considered in detail later in the book. The key to wording these letters is straightforward impersonality. *You* personally are not threatening the reader; rather you are the voice of the system, bringing the system's pressures to bear on the situation—which you know you both want to work out to everyone's satisfaction.

The body of the letter should be single-spaced, with a line space between paragraphs. Paragraphs are normally not indented.

If you use a numbered list, you should separate the entire list from the rest of the body by a line space above and below the list. The list can be ''hang indented,'' that is, the second and following lines (turnovers) of each numbered entry are indented to hang under the opening letter that follows the number:

1. This is a numbered list. Note that the second and following lines of each numbered entry are indented to hang under the first letter that follows the number.
2. This system of hang indents applies to each of the numbered entries in the list. This hang indent format makes reading a numbered list easy.

Do not needlessly repeat yourself. All of us sometimes have a tendency to say the same thing over in other words, just to make sure that the person gets our message. In conversation, we do this when we sense the need for it through watching the reaction of the person to our words. Business letters, however, should make a point clearly and only once. When you've come to the end, end.

The content of the closing paragraph depends in part on how well you know your correspondent. If you know him well, and see him regularly in the course of business, you may wish to end the letter with a personal reference. This letter is not a social note, so this personal reference will not be as personal as a handwritten letter sent to the person's home would be. If your letter lacks a personal note, your correspondent might feel slighted to be treated impersonally and formally. If your letter has this personal note, your correspondent will probably be flattered that you are treating him as a personal friend as well as a business colleague.

Interestingly, the better you know each other and the more you have to deal with each other face to face, the less this personal note need appear. This is so because there are many regular opportunities to affirm the continuance of your friendship. This permits your correspondence to focus only on the business matters.

Any personal references should not be so personal that others might be surprised to see them there. Your secretary and filing personnel will see them—as will your correspondent's. These references will also be read by any who receive photocopies of the letter. They will be read by your correspondent's successor when he reads the file to bring himself up to date. Since the letter is ''public''—between companies—keep in mind that any personal references must be general and innocuous.

Complimentary Closing

The last section of the letter is the complimentary closing. Many business letter writers like to add a transition phrase, so that the letter does not jump immediately from the body to the end. These phrases are usually partial sentences, such as:

`With all kind regards,`

`With all best wishes,`

`With every good wish,`

`With continued regards,`

Sometimes, if the writer is a bit more formal in his manner—and it is clearly a matter of personal style—the phrase "I am" can be added:

`With all kind regards, I am`

`With best wishes, I am`

`With every good wish, I am`

`With continued regards, I am`

This transition phrase is followed by the complimentary closing itself:

`With all kind regards,`

`Sincerely,`

`With every good wish, I am`

`Sincerely yours,`

Complimentary closings include such standard phrases as:

`Sincerely,`

`Sincerely yours,`

`Yours sincerely,`

`Very sincerely yours,`

`Truly yours,`

`Yours truly,`

`Respectfully,`

`Very respectfully,`

The military and the church have elaborate protocols regarding the appropriate complimentary closing when writing up to a superior or down to a subordinate. "Sincerely" alone is always in good taste in business letters, and avoids any suggestion of talking up or down. "Sincerely yours" or "Yours sincerely" are slightly more formal—again a matter of personal taste. "Yours sincerely" is slightly more British. However, most business letter readers would be indifferent to any possible nuances of feeling between "Sincerely," "Sincerely yours," or "Yours sincerely." These readers are far more interested in what you have to say in the body of your letter than in how you close the letter.

Signature and Title

The signature and title lines follow the complimentary closing. Enough room should be left for your signature so that the signature does not look cramped. In fact, it should be surrounded by enough white space to have the appearance of being framed. It is the one place in the letter where your personal mark is made—and indeed, little can be more personal than your signature. So give yourself room to enjoy signing the letter. If the letter needs a second page for just the transition phrase and the complimentary closing, followed by your signature and title, go to the second page for these. Do not break the transition-phrase–closing–signature sequence between two pages.

Your full "official" name should be typed. This is courtesy, since many signatures are hard to decipher. Since you sign only the original copy, a typed name identifies the originator of the letter to all those who receive copies, as well as on your file copy. The official name is that form of your name that you have chosen to use in business.

Even though your official name is typed on the letter, you may choose to sign only your first name or a nickname you use with that reader. If you normally sign only your first name to this particular reader, and then you slip up when signing a stack of letters by signing your official name, your reader may wonder why you have become so formal so suddenly. It is worth taking the few extra seconds to determine how each individual letter should be signed. If the letter you sign improperly is word processed, it is worth having a new copy run out to avoid offending your reader.

Your title is normally typed in the line following your typed name:

Jonathan R. Preston III
National Marketing Manager

This enables the reader—and everyone who receives copies—to know the "position" that is writing the letter, as well as the name of the person who holds that position. The only time it is not appropriate for you to type your title is when that title is included in the printed letterhead. If your name, as well as your title, is printed on the letterhead, there is no need even to type your name under your signature.

Typist's Initials

It is standard business practice to type both the dictator's and the typist's initials following the title line. Often the initials of the dictator or originator are in capitals; the typist's initials are in lower case:

JRP:dlm

JRP/dlm

dlm

This practice serves merely to record who typed the letter. This information may be of use if the letter was typed in a typing pool or handled by a word-processing department. In some offices this practice is declining, since work records are now kept by other methods and there appears to be little reason for noting publicly on the letter who did the typing.

Enclosures

A line after the typist's initials (if they are used) notes that there are enclosures. Ideally, these enclosures should be listed by name. When the letter is given to you to sign, the enclosures should be part of the package, so you can see if everything you want sent is actually there.

If the enclosures are listed by name, the covering letter serves as a record of what was sent:

Enclosures:(1) Agreement for signature
          (2) 1991 Catalog and Price List

Copies

When copies are sent to people, their names should be listed on the letter so everyone who receives a copy of the letter knows who else has also received a copy. The safest manner for listing names is in straight alphabetical order by surname. Usually the official name is used:

```
Michael Konrad
Alicia Montara
Peter D. Schaeffer
```

Some firms use only the last name, together with the appropriate social title:

```
Mr. Konrad
Miss Montara
Dr. Schaeffer
```

And some firms list senior officers first, in order of seniority. To us this seems pretentious and open to awkwardness should the order get mixed up. It is harder to read. Alphabetical listing by official name seems the most logical and the least susceptible to misunderstanding.

A complete business letter in block left format, with all the components, looks like Sample 2.

Sample 2. Standard Business Letter

ABC COMPANY, INC.
123 MAIN STREET
CENTERVILLE, IL 66666

March 17, 1991 ——————— *Date*

John S. Waters, President
XYZ, Inc. ——————— *Address with*
890 Broadway   *company title*
Metropolis, NY 11111

Re: 1992 Fleet Lease —— *Subject*   *Purpose of letter*
                                                           and previous
Dear Mr. Waters: ———— *Salutation*   *Body*   *reference*

Our fleet lease agreement with your company expires on December
31, 1991. It is time for us to get ready for the next leasing
period.
                                                           Discussion

I enclose specifications for our fleet needs for the two-year
lease period, beginning January 1, 1992. Please note that these
specifications call for fifteen (15) automobiles, ranging from
intermediate to luxury models.   *Request or*
                                                  summary

Please prepare a quotation for our consideration. We will make
our decision about the 1992/94 lease on June 15, 1991. We would
appreciate having your quotation no later than June 1, so we can
study it adequately in comparison with others we are seeking.

I have been very pleased with the service your company has given us over the past two leasing periods. I look forward to the possibility of a continued relationship.   — *Personal comments*

With all good wishes, I am —— *Transition*

Sincerely, ———— *Complimentary closing*

Roger F. Brown
President ——— *Name, title*

RFB:amc ———— *Typist's initials*

Enclosure: 1992/94 Lease Specifications —— *Enclosure*

Copies: Michael Konrad
         Alicia Montara ———— *Copies*
         Peter D. Schaeffer

SOME ALTERNATIVE FORMATS

Semiblock

Some firms have the practice of indenting the first line of each paragraph. When this is done, the date, complimentary closing, signature, and title lines are usually indented to just past the center of the page. Paragraph indentations are generally five spaces, although they may be three or four spaces. They may even be ten spaces. This format is known as semiblock. Samples 3 and 4 show variations of the semiblock format.

Sample 3. Semiblock Format (10-space paragraph indentation)

ABC COMPANY, INC.
123 MAIN STREET
CENTERVILLE, IL 66666

March 15, 1989

John S. Waters, President
XYZ, Inc.
890 Broadway
Metropolis, NY 11111

Dear Mr. Waters:

          This is an example of a semiblock format that uses a ten-space paragraph indentation.

The effect of this indentation is to give the letter a somewhat old-fashioned appearance. It hints at a degree of formality that no longer seems appropriate for use in modern business letter writing.

There was a time when all correspondence—including business letters—was written by hand. Since handwritten documents tend to look like a single block of writing on a page, paragraph breaks were marked by deep indentations and large capital letters at the start of each new paragraph. This format provided greater clarity to the reader. However, since typewriters and word processors now produce such clear copy, the device of deep paragraph indentations is no longer a necessity. Its continued use is something of an archaic affectation.

With all good wishes, I remain

Yours sincerely,

Roger F. Brown
President

RFB/amc

Sample 4. Semiblock Format (5-space paragraph indentation)

ABC COMPANY, INC.
123 MAIN STREET
CENTERVILLE, IL 66666

March 15, 1989

John S. Waters, President
XYZ, Inc.
890 Broadway
Metropolis, NY 11111

Dear Mr. Waters:

Paragraphs in this semiblock letter are indented five spaces. The line spacing is single-spaced, and there is a line of space between each of the paragraphs.

The reason for the indentation is to give the letter a more spacious look. It also suggests a slightly more formal atmosphere to the letter than does a block left letter.

This modified semiblock format is suitable for letters from chief executive officers and chairmen of boards, when the letter is a relatively short one.

With all good wishes, I am

Sincerely yours,

Roger F. Brown
President

amc

Address at Base of Letter

Some firms place the address section of the letter at the base of the page rather than immediately after the date line. This is sometimes called the "official style," since the form is used by some government agencies. Sample 5 shows this format.

Sample 5. *Official Style Format*

ABC COMPANY, INC.
123 MAIN STREET
CENTERVILLE, IL 66666

15 March 1989

Dear Mr. Waters:

This is a sample of the official style of business letter format. Not only is it used by some government agencies, but many company officers will use this form when writing a more personal letter.

The reason they choose this style for a more personal letter—one, however, that is written on company letterhead—is that the letter begins immediately with the name of the person to whom the letter is sent.

This letter can be used with the block left style, as in this example. It can also be used with the semiblock style, with paragraphs being indented five spaces.

Sincerely yours,

Roger F. Brown
President

RFB : amc

Mr. John S. Waters
XYZ, Inc.
890 Broadway
Metropolis, NY 11111

One-and-a-half Spacing or Double Spacing

If the letter is a very short one, it will appear lost on a sheet of paper if it is not stretched out by using one-and-a-half spacing or double spacing. One-and-a-half spacing means that there is a half line of space between each line of type; double spacing means that there is a line of space between each line of type. One-and-a-half spacing holds the letter together more. Double spacing is more often used in draft copies only, in order to give room for making written changes in the letter.

Only the body of the letter is given one-and-a-half or double spacing. The rest of the letter's elements are single spaced.

When this extended spacing is used in a letter, paragraphs should normally be indented five spaces. This indentation results in easier reading. Sample 6 shows this format.

Sample 6. One-and-a-half–Spacing Format

ABC COMPANY, INC.
123 MAIN STREET
CENTERVILLE, IL 66666

15 March 1989

John S. Waters, President
XYZ, Inc.
890 Broadway
Metropolis, NY 11111

Dear Mr. Waters:

Our sales force is meeting for its annual sales conference at Paradise Convention Center near Metropolis, July 2–7, 1989.

You and your staff have been so very helpful to us over the past ten years. Our sales people would very much like to meet you and express their thanks personally. Can you come to our sales conference windup banquet at Paradise on July 6? Cocktails are at 6 p.m.

I hope to see you then.

Sincerely,

Roger F. Brown
President

ENVELOPES

Regular Business Envelopes

The majority of business correspondence is sent in No. 10-sized envelopes into which 8½″ × 11″ sheets of letterhead paper can be folded in thirds. The firm's name and address is printed in the upper left-hand corner of the envelope. The addressee's name, firm, and address is typed in the lower right-hand quadrant of the envelope. Sample 7 shows this format.

Sample 7.

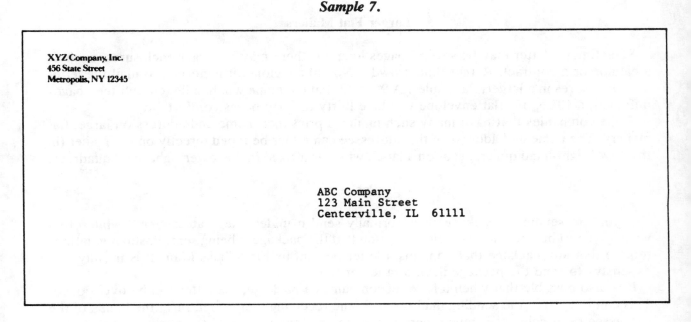

XYZ Company, Inc.
456 State Street
Metropolis, NY 12345

ABC Company
123 Main Street
Centerville, IL 61111

The letter itself may be folded in either of two ways. The more formal and correct method is to use an accordion fold, with the name of the addressee on top.

The more commonly practiced method is to fold the bottom third up and then to fold again to within about one eighth of an inch from the top, with the copy of the letter entirely inside the fold. This method is more common in practice, but less professional in appearance. Sample 8 shows this fold.

Sample 8.

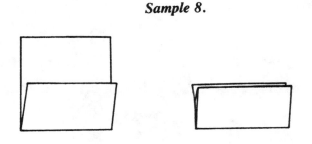

Any small enclosures, such as checks or brochures, should be placed inside the folds. This ensures that they are not "lost" when the letter is taken out. Otherwise, they might be overlooked and thrown away with the envelope. Noting that there is an enclosure with an enclosure line is another caution to the receiver to look in the envelope for the enclosure, should it not be within the fold.

Window Envelopes

Often computer-printed documents, such as statements of accounts and bulk sales or appeal letters, and word processed letters are sent in a window envelope. The firm's name and address is printed in the upper left-hand corner of the envelope. The window, which may or may not have a transparent covering, is in the lower right-hand quadrant. The letter has to have the name and address positioned in such a way that it will appear in the window when the letter is properly folded. Because of its association with monthly statements or bulk sales letters, the window envelope is generally not best suited for business correspondence.

Larger Flat Mailers

Sometimes a letter may be several pages long. Or there may be larger enclosures, such as a catalog or a contract. Rather than crowd a No. 10 envelope, it is normal to mail the letter and enclosures in a larger, flat mailer. A 9″ × 12″ flat envelope will handle ten to fifteen pages unfolded; a 10″ × 13″ flat envelope will take thirty to forty pages comfortably.

Some companies that have many such mailings print their name and address on large, flat mailers. The name and address of the addressee can either be typed directly on the mailer (in the lower right-hand quadrant; or on a label, which is affixed in the lower right-hand quadrant.

Packages

If you are sending a package, you normally send it under "separate cover," while often writing a short business note to tell the person that the package is being sent. Postal regulations require that any package that contains a letter be sent as First-Class Mail. It is usually less expensive to send the package itself at a lesser rate.

It is also possible that when a letter accompanies a package, the letter can be overlooked. This can happen in the sending mail room, in the receiving mail room, or in the hands of the addressee personally. It is much more secure to send the letter and the package separately.

CHAPTER 3

Clear and Unadorned Language

The language used in business correspondence should be clear and unadorned. A business letter is not a literary essay, nor a piece of dramatic prose. It is a straightforward discussion about a basically objective matter. There may be judgment or opinion about the matter, but even such an opinion should be expressed in unemotional terms.

There are guidelines to help a business letter writer use language and grammar in such a way that clarity is preserved but a pleasing style is also maintained. A well-expressed letter makes a far more positive impression on the reader than does an awkwardly phrased, jargon-filled letter.

USE LANGUAGE THAT ACTS

Many business letter writers habitually use passive expressions, such as "it is requested . . . ," "it has come to our attention . . . ," "it is desired . . . ," and the like. These expressions give the feeling that the writer has been acted on rather than being the kind of executive who takes action. As language, these passive statements are weak; as statements, they are evasive and vague.

Direct, action-filled words are stronger. They give a sense that the writer is in control and is dynamically involved with the subject being discussed. "I see that . . . ," "I want you to . . . ," or "I note that . . ." show that the writer interacts with the matter at hand.

"We" should be reserved for a statement about overall company policy or action. The business letter writer should use "I" when stating what he thinks or feels or knows or requests.

Many business executives feel that a large number of syllables are more impressive than few syllables. In fact, many syllables serve to obscure the meaning. The reader gets lost in the maze of long words and often misses the real point of the message. He has to spend so much effort deciphering verbal "noise" that he overlooks the note you are trying to sound.

Bureaucracies, such as government agencies, the military, and educational administrations, are noted for devising complex and lengthy ways of stating relatively simple concepts and procedures. Each business or corporation—which is a bureaucracy of sorts in itself—tends to develop its own jargon. Executives in the company unconsciously adopt this in-house jargon. It soon shows up in their correspondence. And when you use it in correspondence to people outside the company, you require your reader to learn your in-group language in order to know what you are talking about. This places an unfair and unrealistic burden on the reader.

Excessive use of the passive in a business letter signals that the letter is jargon-prone.

Use of the active mode of expression results in shorter, more vigorous sentences and greater vitality throughout the letter. When you write in this active mode, you show yourself to be a take-charge person. Your strength and firmness come through to the reader. Compare these two examples:

```
It has come to our attention that your order of January 17 was misplaced during
our order-handling process. This oversight was due in part to heavy processing
demands that came about because of the holiday season. Immediate action has been
taken to process your order in the most expeditious manner, and it is expected
that you will receive your order in the very near future. It is our intent to
ensure that you will not be inconvenienced in this way in the future.
```

I regret that we temporarily misplaced your January 17 order during the holiday rush. We filled your order today. I appreciate your understanding that an occasional order gets misplaced and assure you we will not make this a habit.

EXPLAIN, BUT DON'T OVEREXPLAIN

You should give your reader reasons for your requests or opinions. These reasons should be the distilled product of a far greater amount of background information. If the reader needs more of the background that supports your approach, he will ask. Don't bore him with it unnecessarily.

If you feel compelled to burden him with more details than he needs or wants, you only confuse matters for him. What's worse, you might cause him to focus on an unessential or even misleading side issue. Keep in mind as you write the letter: Concentrate the reader's attention on the main point; everything else—however much it may interest you or however much you may want to show that you know it—is excess. People are more interested in knowing *what* you have decided than in *how* you reached the decision.

IF YOU CLAIM TOO MUCH, YOU LOSE YOUR CREDIBILITY

One recognized overstatement in your letter raises questions in your reader's mind about all the other statements you make in the letter. If anything, slight understatement is preferable to overstatement.

You want your letter to be taken at face value, with full seriousness. Even if it is a sales letter, claiming too much for your product or your service will cost you your greatest asset—your believability.

Whenever you sense yourself becoming too enthusiastic or too angry or too cautious, be sure to reread the letter and take out any overstatements that may have crept in.

KEEP YOUR LETTER SERIOUS

A business letter is not the place to be a smart aleck or to wisecrack. Resist the temptation, however strong you feel it. Although you may be in a mood when you write the letter in which your flippant remark seems ever so clever, there is no guarantee that your reader will be in any such mood when he receives your letter. Your attempt at humor will most likely be seen as impertinence or ineptness.

Even with someone you know well, it is better to write straightforwardly on the subject; leave the humor for a social occasion when you can readily sense whether your colleague is in the same humorous mood as you.

WRITE IN YOUR OWN STYLE

You have your own natural way of expressing yourself. Use it in your business correspondence. The people who know you will immediately sense that *you* are writing to them—you, the same person they meet elsewhere in the course of your relationship. The people who do not know you personally will still sense that there is a real person behind the letter.

At the same time, recognize that it is always possible to improve the way you write. Everyone learns by copying others; that is how a child learns to talk. The more you have good models for expressing yourself before you, the more that style will become natural to you.

USE THE PARAGRAPH AS YOUR MAIN UNIT OF THOUGHT

A paragraph may consist of a single sentence, although normally there are two or more sentences in a paragraph. There should be, however, only one main thought in the paragraph.

Because business letter readers tend to skim their mail, you should normally make the first sentence in the paragraph the one that expresses the main idea. The rest of the sentences in the paragraph explain, qualify, modify, elaborate, or justify the main point that is made in the paragraph's first sentence.

If you have five topics you want to discuss in a letter about a single main problem, introduce the main problem in the first paragraph, and then talk about one of the subtopics in each of the next five paragraphs. Think of the reader; consider how to make it easiest for him to move with you from one point to the next.

When thinking of the reader, remember how imposing a huge block of type can be. The division of the page into paragraphs aids the reader in taking a mental breather here and there as he moves from paragraph to paragraph. Jamming a great deal into a single, long paragraph generally causes the reader to suffer mental indigestion from trying to take in too much in a single swallow.

At the opposite extreme, too many short paragraphs in rapid succession is also distracting. Ideas come in too staccato a sequence; they are too fast and too disjointed to give the reader time to assimilate them.

SAY THINGS IN A POSITIVE WAY

Some business letter writers unconsciously try to disguise their uncertainty about possible outcomes by ducking behind double negatives such as, "It is not unlikely that . . ."; "it is, however, not inconceivable that . . ."; "it is not without good reason that. . . ." Such convolutions leave the reader in a high state of uncertainty about what you just said. That may be your purpose.

We recommend that you use the negative only to deny something rather than use it as a way to evade making a straightforward comment. Most business letter readers want to be told what is happening or what is going to happen. Even if what is going to happen is that nothing is going to happen, the reader prefers knowing that clearly.

Saying things in a positive way will force you to be more direct, more to the point. It will give you greater conciseness, greater strength. It will ensure that your reader senses that you know what you are about. Conversely, if your letter is filled with uncertainty and ambiguity, your reader will probably come to the conclusion that you are unsure of yourself as an executive.

GENERALLY, STAY WITH STANDARD WORDS

Business life is filled with buzz words—words that enjoy fashion for a time and then fade because of overuse. Each business subgroup has its own jargon. These buzz words are often unintelligible to those outside the subspecialty.

You can communicate with greater certainty if you use standard words—either words that are in common use or words that have an accepted standard meaning in your business—instead of fad words. Your reader will have no doubts about what you mean. If you use fad words, your reader may not know precisely what you intend them to mean. You force him to guess at their meaning. And his guess may be off just enough to misread your meaning.

The use of buzz words as part of your regular business letter vocabulary gives an impression that you are a trendy person, one who may not possess sound business stability. If you wish to convey to your readers that you are reliable, a person of sound judgment and conservative strength, use standard words to express yourself.

Save your buzz words for conversation, where they serve to brighten your speech and show that you are knowledgeable about the latest developments in your field. And in that face-to-face setting, you can clarify your meaning immediately if you sense that communication has broken down over the use of a particular buzz word.

CHOOSE CLARITY INSTEAD OF SHORTCUTS

Every business subgroup has its own shortcut ways of expressing matters it deals with all the time. Accountants talk of "P-and-L's" (profit-and-loss statements), personnel directors about CVs (curricula vitae or résumés), and computer programmers about an IUP (an installed user program). Business organizations and associations are often known by their initials—known, that is, to those people who are routinely involved in their activities.

To avoid the possibility of confusion, use a few additional words in your letter to explain in full. Then, if you wish, put the shortcut in parentheses and use it from that point on in your letter: "The American Bar Association (ABA) will . . . ." This procedure makes it clear to the reader that you are not talking about the American Booksellers Association or the Arizona Brewers Association, when you use the ABA shortcut.

This problem can be especially hard to handle well when you use model numbers. You may be so familiar with the differences between Model 2008C and Model 3812D that you let them roll through your letter in confident cadences. If your reader is a company colleague or a steady customer or a regular vendor who works with these model numbers regularly, you can use the model numbers yourself with clarity, confident that good communication is taking place. If, however, your reader is new to the models, you need to expand your description of them to start with, using terms your reader knows. It may even help to enclose a descriptive brochure of the models under discussion, so there will be no doubt about your meaning.

KEEP YOUR TONE CONSISTENT IN A LETTER

If you start in a formal manner in a letter written to a dignitary, keep the formal manner throughout the letter, even to the complimentary closing. If you are firm at the beginning of a collection letter, do not become informal and personal at the letter's end. If you are solemn and correct in the opening of a condolence letter, do not close it with personal chat.

Your letter should hold together in mood and emotion as well as in substance. When you have decided on the tone you want to use in a letter, use the tone consistently in the letter.

The great majority of business letters today are personal, but with some degree of distance from the reader. As you get to know a particular correspondent better over the course of a business relationship, you can edge closer to friendship in tone. But always keep in mind that it is harder to go back to a more formal relationship after you have gotten closer than it is to retain some distance from the beginning. All too often we let some people in close too quickly, and then we decide we would rather have kept some distance. Reestablishing that distance in the relationship can lead to a business rift that never would have occurred if the distance had been maintained all along. Your business letter tone should be looked on as a part of your business strategy. It is an expression of the business relationship you wish to foster with this particular reader.

CHAPTER 4

Letters For Better Customer Relations

Many letters that you write during the year are aimed at improving customer relations. Every business has customers—those who buy its services and products. Every business has competitors—those who try to assure your customers that they (your competitors) can serve them (your customers) better, faster, cheaper. Even as your sales department is given the charge of getting new and replacement customers for the company, you and all your colleagues are charged with keeping your present customers. Occasional letters are an effective way of reinforcing your best features in the mind of your customers.

Using sales-oriented letters without a strong sales pitch to new and old customers is a sound method of telling the customer that you value him.

WELCOMING A NEW OR POTENTIAL CUSTOMER TO THE COMMUNITY

A new business or family usually receives many printed notices of welcome soon after arriving in a new community. A personal letter with a personal signature will get immediate attention amid the clutter of routine circulars. Such a letter of welcome should be warm in tone, friendly in content, and low-key in any message you wish to convey. The person who receives the letter will always think of you and your company as the one who took the extra effort to write a personal letter in those first days.

TIPS

- Be personal and friendly in tone.
- Sell your services, but do so in a very low-key way.
- Offer some free introductory service or gift (make sure it is not one that creates a sense of obligation in the person).
- Encourage the person to visit your place of business.

Sample 9. Welcoming a New or Potential Customer to the Community I

LONGSHOREMEN'S OYSTER HOUSE
567 FRONT STREET
OCEANSIDE, NJ 09999

March 15, 19XX

XXX XXXXXX XX XXXXXXXXXX
XXXXXXXXXXX
XX XXXXXXX XXX
XXXXXXXXX XX XXXXX

Dear Mr. XXXXXXXXXX:

We at the Longshoremen's Oyster House are pleased to welcome you and your colleagues at XXXXXXXXXXX, Inc., to Oceanside.

The Longshoremen's Oyster House has long been a favorite of Oceanside's business community for seafood lunch and Happy Hour friendship. We hope the MNO people will soon be regulars.

Let us know when you are entertaining clients from out of town and want them to have the finest of fresh local seafood. We'll be most happy to prepare a special dish for the occasion.

Please introduce yourself personally to me when you next visit the Oyster House and enjoy complimentary drinks with your meal.

I look forward to meeting you soon

Cordially yours,

Roger M. Shields
Manager

RMS:nlc

Sample 10. Welcoming a New or Potential Customer to the Community II

ABC COMPANY, INC.
123 MAIN STREET
CENTERVILLE, IL 66666

March 15, 19XX

XXX XXXXXX XX XXXXXXXXXX
XXXXXXXXXXX
XX XXXXXXX XXX
XXXXXXXXX XX XXXXX

Dear Mr. XXXXXXXXXX:

Welcome to Centerville!

How many times in a new community do you wonder how to get in touch with key local services? Please accept the enclosed card of telephone numbers and addresses of such services as a token of our welcome. Many people have found it convenient to tack or tape this card near their telephone.

We hope your need for medication will be limited, but when that need arises, we at ABC Pharmacy stand ready to serve your needs quickly and fully.

We are the only pharmacy in Centerville open until midnight every day of the
year. Sickness takes no holidays; nor does it close early. When you need us, we
are there.

At ABC we use generic drugs to fill your prescription, unless your doctor
prescribes a particular brand. Using generics can save you up to half of what
you would otherwise have to pay, even though the content is identical. This is
another example of ABC's commitment to serve our customer.

Come see us, meet us. Find out which items are on this week's special sale list.
We hope you get into the ABC habit whenever you need a drugstore.

Sincerely,

John P. Rogers
President

amc

WELCOMING A NEW CUSTOMER TO YOUR BUSINESS

It takes but little effort to write a personal letter to a new customer. But this small effort
can pay great dividends in creating customer loyalty. Your services may well be matched by
other firms in town; even pricing is competitive. Such a little thing as being recognized personally early in your relationship may be the key to retaining the person as your customer
regardless of the blandishments of other firms.

Such a letter not only flatters the customer by recognizing him. It also confirms him in his
judgment that he makes sound decisions: The letter shows him that he made a good decision
by placing his business with you and assures him in his opinion that your firm can deliver.
People like to have reinforcement that their judgments are sound.

There is so much bulk mail and there are so many computer-generated statements and appeals
that a personally typed letter is first opened and will be well remembered.

TIPS

- Thank the person for doing business with you.
- Offer some new step to take together.
- Sell a service, but keep the sales low-key.

Sample 11. *Welcoming a New Customer to Your Business I*

ABC COMPANY, INC.
123 MAIN STREET
CENTERVILLE, IL 66666

March 15, 19XX

XXX XXXXXX XX XXXXXXXXXX
XXXXXXXXXXX
XX XXXXXXX XXX
XXXXXXXXX XX XXXXX

Dear Mr. XXXXXXXXXX:

It is such a pleasure to welcome you as a new ABC customer. This marks the beginning of what I hope will be many years of a mutually happy relationship.

I have learned that our customers expect both quality products and quality service. Our staff has been trained to see that you get both without unnecessary delay as standard ABC practice. When you have particular needs for something out of the ordinary or have an especially tight schedule to meet, please let me know so I can personally ensure our best effort.

Normally, John McAdams will service your needs. He will call you monthly as part of our standard service routine to make sure you have your needs fully met for the forthcoming month. Whenever you need to call him for unexpected needs, his private phone number is 123-4567. This will save your having to go through our switchboard.

After reviewing your account information, I have asked John to discuss with you at some convenient time our automatic inventory/reorder software program. This is a software program we supply at actual cost to medium-to-high volume customers to make monitoring of inventory levels and reorder points easier and more accurate. This is a new service and is one we have so far found helps both the customer and us. I believe it would interest you.

Again, welcome to the ABC family. And let me be so bold as to add that we are happy to have been invited to be a part of the XXXXXXXXX, Inc., family!

Sincerely yours,

John P. Rogers
President

JPR/amc

Sample 12. *Welcoming a New Customer to Your Business II*

ABC COMPANY, INC.
123 MAIN STREET
CENTERVILLE, IL 66666

March 15, 19XX

XXX XXXXXX XX XXXXXXXXX
XXXXXXXXXXX
XX XXXXXXX XXX
XXXXXXXXX XX XXXXX

Dear Mr. XXXXXXXXXX:

Thank you for having your first prescription filled at ABC Pharmacy. We are pleased to welcome you as a customer.

I hope you found our service speedy and our staff courteous and efficient. We do far more at ABC than sell drugs; we serve in every way we can.

Please feel free to talk over your needs and interests with our registered pharmacists. We will try to guide you among the wide range of nonprescription medications on the shelves, answering your questions about the products and what they do.

When you bring us your prescription, we try to fill it at once. Please plan to give us a few minutes to register the prescription—both to comply with state law and to be able to fill your needs more efficiently in the future.

May I remind you that we are open every day of the year until midnight.

We have weekly specials on sale, beginning each Monday. Come and browse any time. Now that you've used us once, I hope the experience was so pleasing to you that you'll be an ABC regular customer.

Sincerely,

John P. Rogers
President

amc

HOLIDAY GREETINGS

A holiday season provides a timely occasion to wish your better customers, vendors, or colleagues well. A short personal letter is much more noticed and appreciated than is a routine card. There is no need in such a letter to elaborate. It is best not to use the occasion to try to sell something; a sales pitch in the letter destroys its thoughtful, personal, holiday tone.

TIPS

- Make your message simple and honest.
- Keep sales out of this letter.
- If the holiday is of a religious nature, keep in mind the religious sensibilities of the person.

Sample 13. Holiday Greetings I

ABC COMPANY, INC.
123 MAIN STREET
CENTERVILLE, IL 66666

December 15, 19XX

XXX XXXXXX XX XXXXXXXXXX
XXXXXXXXXXX
XX XXXXXXX XXX
XXXXXXXXX XX XXXXX

Dear Mr. XXXXXXXXXX:

The holiday season is a time to think of family and special friends. We at ABC consider you one of those special people; and we are pleased to think you think of us in the same way. We have had a good year together. Thanks for your part in it.

May you and yours have a joyous holiday season. And may 19XX be the best year yet!

Sincerely,

John P. Rogers
President

amc

Sample 14. Holiday Greetings II

ABC COMPANY, INC.
123 MAIN STREET
CENTERVILLE, IL 66666

December 15, 19XX

XXX XXXXXX XX XXXXXXXXXX
XXXXXXXXXXX
XX XXXXXXX XXX
XXXXXXXXX XX XXXXX

Dear Mr. XXXXXXXXXX:

There are many things I'd like to say at this Christmastime. I'd like to speak of friendship, of thoughtfulness, of goodwill and peace. I'd like to talk of service and helpfulness as a way of life. I'd like to tell you how much I appreciate knowing you.

Perhaps the simplest and most meaningful way to say all the things that are on our hearts this time of year is just to say Merry Christmas and a Happy New Year—from the heart!

May 19XX bring great joy to you and yours.

Sincerely,

John P. Rogers
President

amc

APPRECIATION FOR A GOOD BUSINESS SUGGESTION

One of your customers writes with a suggestion about improving one of your products or services. After considering the merits of the suggestion, you decide to implement it in some way. You should write the customer to express your appreciation to him for making the suggestion. If you wish, you might offer a free sample of the improved product as a tangible expression of your appreciation.

TIPS

- Include some brief explanation of how the suggestion is going to be implemented.
- Be specific about the actual suggestion, so your reader knows he is not just getting a form thank-you letter.

Sample 15. Appreciation for a Good Business Suggestion I

ABC COMPANY, INC.
123 MAIN STREET
CENTERVILLE, IL 66666

March 15, 19XX

XXX XXXXXX XX XXXXXXXXX
XXXXXXXXXXX
XX XXXXXXX XXX
XXXXXXXXX XX XXXXX

Dear Mr. XXXXXXXXXX:

Many thanks for your helpful letter in which you suggested we color code the flexible rods used in assembling our portable windscreen.

We have examined your suggestion carefully and believe it to be most constructive. Our design people are working now on a modification of our present rods that will enable us to implement your suggestion when we manufacture the next supply of rods.

I want you to know how much we appreciate your taking the time and effort to write to us. As a token of our gratitude, I will send you a new windscreen with color—coded rods as soon as they come into stock. According to the way our present inventory is moving, I expect this will be around mid—August.

Again, our thanks. And we hope you will enjoy your present windscreen during the summer season.

Sincerely yours,

John P. Rogers
President

JPR:amc

Sample 16. Appreciation for a Good Business Suggestion II

ABC COMPANY, INC.
123 MAIN STREET
CENTERVILLE, IL 66666

March 15, 19XX

XXX XXXXXX XX XXXXXXXXXX
XXXXXXXXXXX
XX XXXXXXX XXX
XXXXXXXXX XX XXXXX

Dear Mr. XXXXXXXXXX:

Thank you for your helpful suggestion that we place information on our automatic coffee maker about ordering a replacement coffee carafe.

We agree with you that glass carafes break and that it is hard to know how to find a replacement carafe when this happens. We also agree with you that people tend to throw away or lose the instruction booklets, and so lose information about replacement parts.

We have had a decal prepared with a toll-free telephone number to call for parts information. In our next manufacturing cycle, we are placing this decal right on the back of each automatic coffee maker.

As a token of our appreciation for this suggestion, we are sending you an extra carafe in case yours breaks or you want to make an extra pot of coffee for guests.

Thanks again for your very practical suggestion.

Sincerely,

John P. Rogers
President

amc

APPRECIATION FOR A BUSINESS SUGGESTION YOU DID NOT IMPLEMENT

Not all suggestions from customers are usable. Nonetheless, you should write a brief note to thank the person for the suggestion and offer a noncommittal explanation why you are not putting the suggestion into practice. You should avoid getting into much explanation, lest the writer start up correspondence with you further defining his suggestion and defending his insight.

TIPS

- Express your thanks for the suggestion, mentioning it specifically.
- Indicate that your studies (this tells him you have taken his suggestion seriously) have led you to conclude that at this time his suggestion is not going to be implemented.
- Express encouragement without giving undue hope that future suggestions or proposals will be accepted.

Sample 17. Appreciation for a Business Suggestion You Did Not Implement I

ABC COMPANY, INC.
123 MAIN STREET
CENTERVILLE, IL 66666

March 15, 19XX

XXX XXXXXX XX XXXXXXXXXX
XXXXXXXXXXX
XX XXXXXXX XXX
XXXXXXXXX XX XXXXX

Dear Mr. XXXXXXXXXX:

Many thanks for your helpful letter in which you suggested we color code the flexible rods used in assembling our portable windscreen.

We have carefully examined your suggestion and have reluctantly concluded that at the present time we are unable to put your suggestion into practice. We are, however, keeping it on file for future consideration should we redesign our windscreen product.

We appreciate the good words you said about the windscreen and are grateful you took the time and effort to encourage us to improve it. Loyal and helpful customers like you are the reason we stay in business. Thank you so much for writing.

Yours sincerely,

John P. Rogers
President

JPR/amc

Sample 18. Appreciation for a Business Suggestion You Did Not Implement II

ABC COMPANY, INC.
123 MAIN STREET
CENTERVILLE, IL 66666

March 15, 19XX

XXX XXXXXX XX XXXXXXXXX
XXXXXXXXXXX
XX XXXXXXX XXX
XXXXXXXXX XX XXXXX

Dear Mr. XXXXXXXXXX:

Thank you for your suggestion that we place information on our automatic coffee makers about ordering a replacement carafe.

We have recently reorganized our sales and services procedures. We will be supplying every dealer who sells our coffee makers with a small supply of replacement carafes. We also will provide each dealer with complete instructions on ordering any part of our inventory.

By making replacement a dealer function, we trust that service to our customers will be more personal and effective.

Thank you again for your suggestion. We appreciate loyal customers like you and hope to serve you better year by year.

Sincerely,

John P. Rogers
President

amc

APPRECIATION FOR A FAVOR

Part of conducting business is doing a favor for a business colleague from time to time. And sometimes you have to ask for a favor. You should always write a short note to express your thanks when a favor is done for you.

TIPS

- Mention the favor by name and express in some way that you were in fact helped by it.
- Indicate that you will be happy to help your reader in some way in the future.

Sample 19. Appreciation for a Favor I

ABC COMPANY, INC.
123 MAIN STREET
CENTERVILLE, IL 66666

March 15, 19XX

XXX XXXXXX XX XXXXXXXXXX
XXXXXXXXXXX
XX XXXXXXX XXX
XXXXXXXXX XX XXXXX

Dear Mr. XXXXXXXXXX:

Thank you so much for suggesting an ad agency for us to look into. The quality
and effectiveness of your own ads is what led us to approach you for your
suggestions.

We have since concluded an arrangement with the agency you suggested for a two-
year campaign. We are quite thrilled about the approaches they have taken in
dramatizing our product and bringing to our attention new markets we had not
considered.

If there is some way we can ever return your kindness, please let me know. I
would be most happy to be of some help to you.

Sincerely yours,

John P. Rogers
President

amc

Sample 20. Appreciation for a Favor II

ADS GALORE
678 FRONT STREET
CENTERVILLE, IL 66666

March 15, 19XX

XXX XXXXXX XX XXXXXXXXX
XXXXXXXXXXX
XX XXXXXXX XXX
XXXXXXXXX XX XXXXX

Dear Mr. XXXXXXXXXX:

Thank you for suggesting to John P. Rogers of the ABC Company that he consider using us as ABC's ad agency. You will be pleased to know that we have just concluded a contract to serve him for the next two years. He seems quite pleased with the campaign we have outlined for him.

We could never grow without references from loyal clients. We are pleased to count you as first among our most valued clients. Please let me know if there is some way I can return the kindness you have shown us.

With much appreciation, I am

Yours sincerely,

Mario Gallento

MG:mlr

ACKNOWLEDGMENT OF RECEIPT OF A LETTER

Generally, a letter can be answered soon after it arrives. There are times, however, that a delay will occur before the letter can be properly considered. It is courteous to drop a short letter to the writer just to let him know that his letter has arrived. It is very aggravating to write a company and feel that you have been ignored.

TIPS

- Be specific about the letter you are acknowledging. This reassures the reader that it is his letter you are writing about.
- Note what action is being taken about the letter at the present time. This shows the reader that his letter is not on ''indefinite hold.''
- Explain briefly why there is not yet a full response to his question. Explain as little as possible without being brusque.

Sample 21. Acknowledgment of Receipt of a Letter I

ABC COMPANY, INC.
123 MAIN STREET
CENTERVILLE, IL 66666

March 15, 19XX

XXX XXXXXX XX XXXXXXXXX
XXXXXXXXXXX
XX XXXXXXX XXX
XXXXXXXXX XX XXXXX

Dear Mr. XXXXXXXXXX:

Thank you for your letter of March 3 in which you submit a proposal regarding a distributorship of our sports line in the southeastern states.

Mr. George Marshall, our national marketing manager, handles our distributorship arrangements. Mr. Marshall is overseas on a well—earned vacation for the rest of this month. He will be in touch with you during the first half of June after his return to the office.

With every good wish, I am

Sincerely yours,

John P. Rogers
President

Copy: George Marshall

amc

Sample 22. Acknowledgment of Receipt of a Letter II

ABC COMPANY, INC.
123 MAIN STREET
CENTERVILLE, IL 66666

March 15, 19XX

XXX XXXXXX XX XXXXXXXXXX
XXXXXXXXXXX
XX XXXXXXX XXX
XXXXXXXXX XX XXXXX

Dear Mr. XXXXXXXXXX:

Thank you for your March 10 letter in which you ask for information about our
Page Organizer software program.

I have forwarded your letter to Hal Johnson, our field representative for your
area. Mr. Johnson will call you during the last half of this month to explain
Page Organizer's features and cost. If it appears that Page Organizer will meet
your needs, Mr. Johnson will make arrangements for a demonstration at your
convenience.

Sincerely,

John P. Rogers
President

amc

Copy: Hal Johnson

APPRECIATION FOR A COMPLIMENTARY LETTER ABOUT AN EMPLOYEE

When someone takes the time and effort to write a letter complimenting one of your employees, you should also take the time and effort to express your appreciation to that customer.
People are so much more prone to write when they are angry and wish to lodge a complaint.
When they write because they are pleased with your company, be sure you reinforce their
good feelings by a prompt response.

TIPS

- If ever a letter should be personal, this one should be. But don't overdo it.
- The writer not only wants to thank the company, he also wants to feel that the employee
  who was so helpful is recognized by the company. Your letter should make it clear that
  the employee is being so recognized.
- A low-key hope for continued business support is quite in order.

Sample 23. Appreciation for a Complimentary Letter About an Employee I

ABC COMPANY, INC.
123 MAIN STREET
CENTERVILLE, IL 66666

March 15, 19XX

XXX XXXXXX XX XXXXXXXXXX
XXXXXXXXXXX
XX XXXXXXX XXX
XXXXXXXXX XX XXXXX

Dear Mr. XXXXXXXXXX:

Thank you for your thoughtful letter of February 24 in which you bring to my
attention the pleasing and helpful way you were served by Jane Creighton, our
customer relations specialist.

We are always most pleased to receive a letter that commends one of our staff. It
provides us with continued evidence that our people take the extra steps to
ensure that your specific needs are understood and met. In addition to my own
expression of appreciation to Ms Creighton, you can be sure that her immediate
supervisor will also commend her for this job well done.

We have every confidence that you will continue to find our staff courteous and
helpful, and we look forward to serving you regularly in the years ahead.

Sincerely yours,

John P. Rogers
President

JPR/amc

Copy: Jane Creighton

Sample 24. *Appreciation for a Complimentary Letter About an Employee II*

ABC COMPANY, INC.
123 MAIN STREET
CENTERVILLE, IL 66666

March 15, 19XX

XXX XXXXXX XX XXXXXXXXXX
XXXXXXXXXXX
XX XXXXXXX XXX
XXXXXXXXX XX XXXXX

Dear Mr. XXXXXXXXXX:

Thank you for your March 10 letter in which you express how helpful Tom Readman was to you during last month's blackout emergency.

Tom loves his work, enjoys his customers, and lives by an inner drive that requires him to go the extra mile. We are most fortunate to have Tom on our staff. It is a pleasure to be able to send such an able person to serve a customer.

I'm sending a copy of your letter to Tom and placing one in his personnel file.

We hope you don't have reason to call on Tom often, but when you do, we know he'll get your equipment back on line quickly and efficiently.

Sincerely,

John P. Rogers
President

amc

Copy: Tom Readman

ADJUSTMENT MADE

In every business there are times customers complain about a matter in which the company is in error or for which it is willing to take responsibility. An adjustment is to be made in the customer's favor. It is good business practice to write a letter to the customer, acknowledging that the customer's position was correct and indicating what steps the company is taking to set the matter right. It is not necessary to go into a long explanation of what broke down or to try to assign responsibility. The customer does not really care about the details of your internal problems or structure; he only wants the matter resolved in his favor. A letter can help turn a disgruntled customer into a loyal one who will sing your praises by word of mouth.

TIPS

- Keep the mood of your letter positive. If it seems to the customer that you are reluctantly giving in, the positive steps you have taken to rectify the situation will be nullified by what appears to be a mean spirit.
- Even though you may acknowledge responsibility, don't overapologize. By retaining your dignity, you keep the customer's respect.
- Make it clear what steps you are taking to set the matter right; don't allow the customer to expect more than you are going to do. Avoid vagueness on this point.
- Make it clear as well that you do not expect the same problems to arise in the future.

Sample 25. Adjustment Made I

ABC COMPANY, INC.
123 MAIN STREET
CENTERVILLE, IL 66666

March 15, 19XX

XXX XXXXXX XX XXXXXXXXXX
XXXXXXXXXXX
XX XXXXXXX XXX
XXXXXXXXX XX XXXXX

Dear Mr. XXXXXXXXXX:

Thank you for your letter of March 3 in which you report that three of the glass spice jars we sent you were broken in transit.

We're glad the other nine arrived safely, and we hope you have already put them to good use. In the meantime, we have sent you three replacement jars by express service. We apologize for any inconvenience this problem may have caused you.

Our packing department is well-trained in secure shipping procedures. Damage en route is very rare. We trust you will continue to order from our wide range of gourmet foods and supplies with every confidence that your orders will arrive promptly and intact.

Sincerely,

Mary S. Chilvers
Customer Service

MSC/jb

Sample 26. Adjustment Made II

ABC COMPANY, INC.
123 MAIN STREET
CENTERVILLE, IL 66666

March 15, 19XX

XXX XXXXXX XX XXXXXXXXXX
XXXXXXXXXXX
XX XXXXXXX XXX
XXXXXXXXX XX XXXXX

Dear Mr. XXXXXXXXXX:

Thank you for your March 10 letter in which you indicate that both the ladies'
and men's shorts you ordered are too small.

As you know, different manufacturers use different patterns when making
clothes. Some models are cut to a slightly fuller cut than others, even though
the size is the same, and some are cut to a slightly smaller cut. It's a matter of
cut within the size range as well as the size itself.

The cuts (and hence the sizes) on these shorts do appear to run tight. We will be
pleased either to replace your shorts with the next larger size or to refund
your purchase. Since you purchased by credit card, we would credit your account
with the amount of the purchase plus shipping.

Please return the shorts with a note, giving us your directions. If you like the
shorts, we suggest you try the next larger size.

We are grateful for your patronage and always stand ready to serve you.

Sincerely,

John P. Rogers
President

amc

ADJUSTMENT DENIED

There are also some times when a customer's request for an adjustment has to be denied.
It is harder to keep that person as a customer when this occurs, but a gracious letter can help
do so. The key is not to make the customer feel that he is considered overdemanding in making
his request, but to assure him that his complaint has been seriously considered. A brief but
reasonable answer as to why his request is denied is essential in keeping his loyalty.

TIPS

- Help the customer sense that you really understand his position. Nothing is worse than to be denied for the "wrong" reason: That compounds your faults in the customer's eyes.
- Explain why you are not granting his request, but do so in plain words. Avoid ambiguous jargon that might give the customer the feeling you are trying to avoid his question. A straightforward "no" is much easier to accept than a vague reassurance.

Sample 27. Adjustment Denied I

ABC COMPANY, INC.
123 MAIN STREET
CENTERVILLE, IL 66666

March 15, 19XX

XXX XXXXXX XX XXXXXXXXXX
XXXXXXXXXXX
XX XXXXXXX XXX
XXXXXXXXX XX XXXXX

Dear Mr. XXXXXXXXXX:

We were sorry to hear that the cam for your Mor-Sew sewing machine has broken. We regret to report that our firm sold the Mor-Sew Company two years ago and that under the new owner the company no longer makes sewing machines.

We supplied the new owner with all available spare parts we had at the time of purchase, but we cannot tell what parts are now available.

I suggest you write to:

       Macrotex Industries
       10012 Industrial Boulevard
       Memphis, TN 00000

and include the model number of your Mor-Sew machine, together with a description of the parts you need.

We regret that we are now unable to help you and hope you will be able to secure the part you need elsewhere.

Sincerely,

George T. McDonnell
Vice President

GTM:ec

Sample 28. Adjustment Denied II

ABC COMPANY, INC.
123 MAIN STREET
CENTERVILLE, IL 66666

March 15, 19XX

XXX XXXXXX XX XXXXXXXXXX
XXXXXXXXXXX
XX XXXXXXX XXX
XXXXXXXXX XX XXXXX

Dear Mr. XXXXXXXXXX:

Thank you for your March 10 letter requesting repair without charge of your 19XX Model 759 automatic coffee maker, serial number 1001015-X.

We regret that there are two problems in granting your request:

1. The particular coffee maker was never registered under our warranty plan. For whatever reason this registration was not made, our plan calls for such a registration in order for the warranty to be in effect.
2. Even had the registration of the coffee maker been made, the period of warranty is long since past. We provided a one-year warranty on all Model 759 coffee makers; but Model 759 went out of production eight years ago. Unless you have a sales slip that shows you purchased the coffee maker within the past year, we would not even be able to waive our registration rule to provide service without charge.

You think that the heating element has failed. May I suggest that it would be more expensive to have that element replaced in an appliance repair shop than it would be to buy a new coffee maker.

We hope you will buy an ABC coffee maker. I'm enclosing a brochure that describes our current line. And I urge you, whatever brand you purchase, to send in your warranty registration card soon after your purchase.

If you enjoyed your Model 759, we know you'll love our current line.

Sincerely,

John P. Rogers
President

amc

THANKS FOR A DIFFICULT JOB DONE WELL

At times there are difficult jobs to be done quickly and well or complex jobs to be completed by a deadline that places great pressure on people. Sometimes these jobs are done by people in your company; sometimes they are performed by an outside vendor or service. A letter from senior management that recognizes the excellent performance and expresses thanks will help cement a spirit of loyalty. People need to be recognized.

TIPS

- When you thank the person, the people, or the company for the job, be specific about what you appreciated. This shows the reader that you have looked at the work, assessed its difficulty, and concluded that the reader's work was beyond normal expectations.
- Express some way in which this effort did something for you or the company that would not otherwise have happened.
- Don't overdo your thanks. You will probably need to call on these people time and again for extra efforts, so put your thanks into a context of ongoing relations of superior work.

Sample 29. Thanks for a Difficult Job Done Well I

ABC COMPANY, INC.
123 Main Street
Centerville, IL 66666

March 15, 19XX

XXX XXXXXX XX XXXXXXXXXX
XXXXXXXXXXX
XX XXXXXXX XXX
XXXXXXXXX XX XXXXX

Dear Mr. XXXXXXXXXX:

As you know, from one point of view a computer system is no better than the field engineer who services it. And in Martin Donovan you have one of the finest we have ever seen.

Our business depends on our being able to meet deadlines. Late last Wednesday afternoon the system crashed and we put in an emergency call to your office. Mr. Donovan came at once, accurately diagnosed the problem, phoned for the proper replacement parts, waited until they arrived, and stayed on into the late night getting the system up and running again. Because of his extraordinary efforts, we made our deadline.

We want both you and Mr. Donovan to know how much we value his ability and his wonderful spirit when faced with a tough job.

With every good wish, I remain

Sincerely yours,

John P. Rogers
President

Copy: Martin Donovan

amc

Sample 30. *Thanks for a Difficult Job Done Well II*

ABC COMPANY, INC.
123 Main Street
Centerville, IL 66666

March 15, 19XX

XXXXX X. XXXXXXXXX
ABC Company, Inc.
123 Main Street
Centerville, IL 66666

Dear XXXXXX:

This is to thank you for the superb job you and your crew did in running the company exhibit at the annual exhibitors' convention.

The exhibit looked terrific. It was always manned. Your people were pleasant and knowledgeable. Even though the main purpose of the convention is not to write orders, our people wrote three times the business we have ever had before at a convention.

With this kind of effort, no wonder 19XX is shaping up to be our best year ever.

Please convey my personal thanks to everyone in your department who made the convention such a success.

Sincerely,

John P. Rogers
President

amc

GENERAL THANK-YOU LETTER

A good business suggestion is to plan to write two thank-you letters a week. Most business executives feel they are too pressed for time to write a short letter of thanks, yet few actions are more appreciated. The best way to develop the art of writing thank-you letters is to build the practice into your regular routine. One hundred such letters take very little time when they are spread out over the course of the year, but they add up to an impressive number of associates who feel far more positive toward you and your company than would otherwise have been true. This letter is a solid relation builder.

TIPS

- Be specific in telling the reader what you are thanking him for. He is probably not expecting a letter from you on business, so this letter will come as a pleasant surprise.
- Be generous in your thanks, but also be restrained. You don't want to embarrass him by overdoing it.
- Tell your reader that you look forward to seeing him again and that you hope it will be soon.

Sample 31. General Thank-you Letter I

ABC COMPANY, INC.
123 MAIN STREET
CENTERVILLE, IL 66666

March 15, 19XX

XXX XXXXXX XX XXXXXXXXXX
XXXXXXXXXXX
XX XXXXXXX XXX
XXXXXXXXX XX XXXXX

Dear Mr. XXXXXXXXXX:

Thank you so much for your note regarding the award that the national association presented to me at the annual dinner last week.

One of the nicest things about such an event is the way it brings one in touch with old and valued friends. The award is momentary; the friendships are lasting. Your own kind words mean a great deal to me.

I was pleased to learn that your youngest, Robert, is now finishing college. I can recall when he first entered kindergarten. How proud you must be of all your children. We should get together and compare notes on how to handle the empty-nest syndrome. With our kids all away for good (we think), Annette and I are at a similar stage in our passage in life.

I hope to be in your town next month. I'll call to see if we can have lunch together and catch up on things.

Sincerely,

John P. Rogers
President

JPR:amc

Sample 32. General Thank-you Letter II

ABC COMPANY, INC.
123 MAIN STREET
CENTERVILLE, IL 66666

March 15, 19XX

XXX XXXXXX XX XXXXXXXXX
XXXXXXXXXXX
XX XXXXXXX XXX
XXXXXXXXX XX XXXXX

Dear Mr. XXXXXXXXXX:

It was so very kind of you to drive me to the airport at the end of the meeting last week. I know how inconvenient it was for you in the midst of such a storm. I do hope your family was not overly worried about your safety on the way home at that late hour.

I was happy at the opportunity of getting to know you more personally during that rather memorable drive. There are all too many times in life that the only association we have with colleagues is over a committee table or across a desk. I have come to admire your capabilities in those business settings, and I am pleased now to have this more personal association.

Thanks again for getting me to the plane on time. I look forward to seeing you again at the next meeting.

Sincerely,

John P. Rogers
President

JPR/amc

LETTER OF APOLOGY

Sometimes there is nothing you can do but apologize. You may or may not have a good reason for what happened—or didn't happen. If there is a reason that can be stated in a few words, state it without trying to hide. If there is no good reason, admit things got out of hand. Your reader will probably remember times he was in a similar situation and will be quite willing to accept your apology in spirit as well as in fact.

TIPS

- Accept the fact that you need to apologize. Don't try to defend or justify yourself.
- Apologize simply and in a few words. Avoid overdramatizing your failure.
- Assure the reader that you will do better in the future, if such assurance is called for.

Sample 33. Letter of Apology I

ABC COMPANY, INC.
123 MAIN STREET
CENTERVILLE, IL 66666

March 15, 19XX

XXX XXXXXX XX XXXXXXXXXX
XXXXXXXXXXX
XX XXXXXXX XXX
XXXXXXXXX XX XXXXX

Dear Mr. XXXXXXXXXX:

Please accept my apology for not sending you the estimate on the Barkan job on time.

One can always say our system went down at the worst possible time, but I know you are far more interested in having the estimate in a timely manner than in hearing about our last-minute problems. It was most embarrassing to discover that it was your work that was delayed; I have taken steps to ensure it receives the highest priority in the future.

The estimate has been sent by express delivery and you should have it in hand now. Please call with any questions.

I look forward to serving you properly on the Barkan job.

Sincerely,

John P. Rogers
President

amc

Sample 34. Letter of Apology II

ABC COMPANY, INC.
123 MAIN STREET
CENTERVILLE, IL 66666

March 15, 19XX

XXX XXXXXX XX XXXXXXXXX
XXXXXXXXXXX
XX XXXXXXX XXX
XXXXXXXXX XX XXXXX

Dear Mr. XXXXXXXXXX:

How embarrassing to have missed the board meeting last night. Please accept my apology for this almost unforgivable oversight.

I worked late on an emergency that cropped up at the end of the day. Rather than double—check my appointment book, I rather automatically followed Wednesday routine—still thinking about that emergency. It was only this morning that I looked at my book and realized that I had completely overlooked the meeting.

I've got the next board meeting circled in red and assure you I'll be there.

Sincerely,

John P. Rogers
President

amc

ANNIVERSARY OF AN EMPLOYEE

It is good business practice to keep a record of significant employee anniversaries: one year, five years, ten years, fifteen years, and so on. An executive can ask the personnel department to notify him of the anniversaries of staff members who work with him prior to their happening. The employee or colleague will be very pleased to have been remembered; in fact, your letter may serve to remind him of the anniversary.

TIPS

- Be personal, but not overly sentimental.
- Mention something specific about the employee's work or contribution for which you are appreciative.
- If you are writing to a peer, mention some shared experience from which you have profited or the company has benefited.

Sample 35. Anniversary of an Employee I

ABC COMPANY, INC.
123 MAIN STREET
CENTERVILLE, IL 66666

March 15, 19XX

XXX XXXXXX XX XXXXXXXXX
XXXXXXXXXXX
XX XXXXXXX XXX
XXXXXXXX XX XXXXX

Dear XXXXXXXXX:

Although it's been ten years since you started work with ABC, it seems like only
a couple of years ago that you came to us as a raw, inexperienced field
representative. I well remember those early days of visiting you in the
Southwest Region and talking over how best to handle difficult accounts during
our changeover to centralized order fulfillment. And I remember how quickly you
learned and how loyal those customers have been during the years since.

From field rep to regional sales manager to national sales manager to marketing
director—all in just under ten years. You've done well for the company, and the
company is proud of your record.

May you go from strength to strength for the next ten years! It's one of the nice
things in life that's happened to me to have you as a colleague.

As ever,

Sincerely,

John P. Rogers
President

JPR:amc

Sample 36. *Anniversary of an Employee II*

ABC COMPANY, INC.
123 MAIN STREET
CENTERVILLE, IL 66666

March 15, 19XX

XXX XXXXX XX XXXXXXXXX
XXXXXXXXXX
XX XXXXXX XXX
XXXXXXXX XX XXXXX

Dear Mrs. XXXXXXXXX:

All of us at ABC congratulate you on the occasion of completing twenty years of faithful service.

In these days of constant change, such a long period of service is rare. We are pleased you have found ABC to be the kind of company that you want to be associated with over the years; and we assure you that we have greatly appreciated your loyalty and contribution to the firm. We especially are grateful that you stayed with us throughout those difficult days seven years ago when even the existence of the company was in question. What a wonderful change for the better we have all seen since then.

I know the folks in the quality control section are hosting a little luncheon for you today. I only wish I could be there to add my personal "Thanks and best wishes" to theirs, but I must unfortunately be out of town. So please let this, in my absence, convey my heartiest thanks.

May we enjoy many more years together.

Sincerely,

John P. Rogers
President

amc

ANNIVERSARY OF A FIRM

Firms—as well as individuals—celebrate anniversaries. They tend to promote their anniversary at quarter-century intervals. If one of your customers or suppliers is celebrating such an occasion, a letter from you will help cement relationships.

TIPS

- Express your congratulations with sincerity and dignity.
- Include some reference to ways in which your two firms have benefited from the relationship.
- Wish the firm well for another anniversary period.

Sample 37. Anniversary of a Firm I

ABC COMPANY, INC.
123 MAIN STREET
CENTERVILLE, IL 66666

March 15, 19XX

XXX XXXXXX XX XXXXXXXXXX
XXXXXXXXXXX
XX XXXXXXX XXX
XXXXXXXXX XX XXXXX

Dear Mr. XXXXXXXXXX:

We at ABC congratulate you at XYZ on your fifty years of business enterprise.

I read your anniversary folder with considerable interest. It is quite an accomplishment for a firm to change and grow with the times as yours has. From home ice boxes and ice delivery to industrial coolers and refrigerators is a twentieth-century story to be proud of. I only hope we can adjust to changing times with as much alacrity in our field of business.

Although we have been associated with you for only one tenth of your corporate life, we have found those five years to be helpful and profitable to us.

May the success of your first fifty years be the foundation for an even more successful second fifty.

Sincerely,

John P. Rogers
President

JPR/amc

Sample 38. Anniversary of a Firm II

ABC COMPANY, INC.
123 MAIN STREET
CENTERVILLE, IL

March 15, 19XX

XXX XXXXXX XX XXXXXXXXXX
XXXXXXXXXXX
XX XXXXXX XXX
XXXXXXXXX XX XXXXX

Dear XXXXXXXXXX:

In looking through our records the other day, I realized that this week marks an anniversary of our doing business together.

It was five years ago that we accepted your first bid for advertising services. During these past five years, you have helped put us in the top 10 percent of companies in our field. Not bad for a struggling ad agency and a business that began in a two-room office on the second story. We've done well by each other.

And may the next five years of our relationship be as happy and as productive.

Thanks for learning about us so thoroughly and for communicating what we are so effectively.

Sincerely,

John P. Rogers
President

amc

APOLOGY FOR AN EMPLOYEE'S ATTITUDE OR ACTION

Not every employee is a model employee, and even the best may have an occasional off day. Or a customer may rub an employee in a way that creates conflict and then the customer writes to complain. A tactful letter may turn a dissatisfied customer into one who continues to think well of your company.

TIPS

- Thank the writer for bringing the problem to your attention. You may not know of some problems unless you learn of them through such correspondence.
- Apologize only for the specific problem that has been raised.

- Give the writer a general idea of what kind of action you are taking in correcting the situation so that he has a sense that his letter has proved effective.
- Ask for continued business support.

Sample 39. *Apology for an Employee's Attitude or Action I*

ABC COMPANY, INC.
123 MAIN STREET
CENTERVILLE, IL 66666

March 15, 19XX

XXX XXXXXX XX XXXXXXXXXX
XXXXXXXXXXX
XX XXXXXXX XXX
XXXXXXXXX XX XXXXX

Dear XXXXXXXXXX:

Thank you for your March 10 letter in which you point out how disturbed you were by the attitude of one of our sales clerks, Joan Adams, who seemingly was more interested in conducting a personal telephone conversation than in being of service.

We discussed the matter with Ms Adams, and she acknowledged that she has been trying to resolve some personal matters during the past few weeks and has used the floor phone often in her attempt to do so. This discussion enabled us to have a mutually helpful conversation on the place of private matters in business life. We believe that Ms Adams now has a clearer understanding of what is expected of her and is a better employee for the experience.

She has asked me to convey her apologies to you. I also am sorry that you were not properly cared for when you were in the store. I do thank you for bringing the matter to my attention. I assure you that Ms Adams and any other of our floor staff are committed, as I am, to service.

I hope you will visit us soon.

Sincerely,

John P. Rogers
President

amc

Sample 40. *Apology for an Employee's Attitude or Action II*

ABC COMPANY, INC.
123 MAIN STREET
CENTERVILLE, IL 66666

March 15, 19XX

XXX XXXXXX XX XXXXXXXXX
XXXXXXXXXXX
XX XXXXXXX XXX
XXXXXXXXX XX XXXXX

Dear XXXXXXXXXX:

I was distressed to receive your March 10 letter about the curtness of our telephone sales representative.

I looked into the matter and found out that the representative in question was in the process of leaving our company to enter a new field. You happened to get him on his final day. I can only imagine he felt little sense of responsibility and allowed himself to get into an argument with you.

I apologize for his behavior. There is no corrective action I can take, since he no longer works here.

We have, however, intensified the training and supervision of our telephone sales staff. I'm sure you will find them courteous, knowledgeable, and helpful whenever you call.

And I hope you'll call us again soon.

Sincerely,

John P. Rogers
President

amc

CHAPTER 5

General Letters

Every executive faces various kinds of general correspondence. One is formal letters related to official occasions. Another is responding to letters that a customer, client, or vendor has sent. Another is writing on one's own regarding a business matter. Sometimes these letters in which you take the initiative should be somewhat formal; sometimes they can be more personal. But they should always maintain a sense of dignity. The right blend of business and informality is based in part on the nature of your relationship to the person to whom you are writing. The better you know the person, the more informal your letter can be. In order to judge what is the best tone, ask yourself the following questions: What is the nature of our relationship personally? How much difference is there in our ages? What is the subject I am writing about?

LETTER OF INTRODUCTION

A letter of introduction is a routine part of business correspondence, even though most introductions are made in person or by telephone. You may handle a letter of introduction in any one of several settings. The person who is being introduced may actually carry the letter (the letter may be addressed to a specific addressee or it may be general in nature), or you may send the letter by mail ahead of the person. The letter may be placed in an unsealed envelope, or it may be of a confidential nature and placed in a sealed envelope. The purpose of a letter of introduction is to pave the way positively for the person being introduced.

TIPS

- Give the basic information in the letter: the name of the person, his title or function, and the reason for the introduction.
- If the situation will include personal as well as business relationships, mention one or two personal interests that the addressee and the person being introduced might share in common. The purpose of this is to help lay the groundwork for some point of mutuality other than just the formal business association.
- Show appreciation for any kindness that may be extended to the person being introduced.
- If the introduction is primarily one to help ease a business acquaintance into a new social setting rather than serve as a business introduction, make that point clear from the start.

Sample 41. Letter of Introduction I

ABC COMPANY, INC.
123 MAIN STREET
CENTERVILLE, IL 66666

March 15, 19XX

XXXXX X. XXXXXXXXX
XXXX XXXXXXXXXX XXX.
XXXXXXXXXX, XX XXXXX

Dear XXXXXXXXXXX:

This is to introduce William Gravely, a research pharmacologist at State University.

I've enjoyed knowing Bill Gravely for several years, mostly through membership in a local country club. Bill has a great sense of humor, can tell a wonderful story at the drop of a hat, and goes hot air ballooning for relaxation.

Bill is planning to spend a couple of months in your area later this spring on a study trip for the university. He tells me he wants to speak with some of the Southeast Asian refugees who have settled in your part of the country in order to assess the pharmacological worth of some of the herbs used in their traditional medicines. Anything you can do to put him in touch with one or two of the key social agencies that have contact with these groups would be much appreciated. Bill is using his university connections to make some initial contacts, but would be grateful for any additional ones you might be able to provide. He'll call you after he settles in.

Also, I'm sure Bill would respond to an invitation for an evening out sometime during his stay. I think you'd hit it off well together.

Thanks so much for anything you can do. Please say hello to Ruth.

Sincerely,

John P. Rogers
President

amc

Sample 42. Letter of Introduction II

ABC COMPANY, INC.
123 MAIN STREET
CENTERVILLE, IL 66666

March 15, 19XX

XXXXX X. XXXXXXXXXX
XXXXXXXXXXXX XX.
XXXX XXXXXXXXXX XXX.
XXXXXXXXXX, XX XXXXX

Dear XXXXXXXXXX:

In early June you will receive a call from Martin Owens to set up an appointment with you.

Mr. Owens is our new systems analyst. His main task is to determine how we can best upgrade the services we offer our major clients. Right now he is studying your present application of our systems program in order to have a sound basis for any future development.

In June he hopes to go over with your people what you project your systems needs might be during the next three years. His aim is twofold: (1) to improve the efficiency and turnaround in the present processing as well as to simplify entry procedures at your end, and (2) to anticipate any new requirements you might have and prepare for them in a way that will not cause any disturbance in ongoing processing.

You will find Mr. Owens to be highly knowledgeable both in data processing and in practical business procedures and possibilities. We are very pleased that he has come to us and are confident you will find him easy and pleasant to work with. But even more important, we know you will be pleased at the down-to-earth way he can help resolve systems problems without creating greater ones while doing so.

Continued good wishes,

Sincerely,

John P. Rogers
President

JPR:amc

LETTER OF RECOMMENDATION

Every executive is asked from time to time for a letter of recommendation regarding a former employee. The letter may be requested directly by the former employee, or it may be requested by the firm that is considering hiring the former employee. If the former employee is to take the letter personally, it is courteous to deliver the letter to the former employee in an unsealed envelope. A letter of recommendation written to the personnel director or other officer of the enquiring company is usually marked "Confidential" and sealed in a separate envelope.

You should not recommend a person enthusiastically unless you can do so without reservation. If you have reservations about the person's qualifications or character, you should comment on what is positive about the person and avoid commenting in the areas where you have questions even though you were specifically asked about them. Since under federal and state "sunshine" laws, most employee records are available to the employee for review, you should take care not to make negative statements about the former employee that could be the basis for legal action against you. You may decide it is better just to decline to write a letter.

The reader of your letter of recommendation looks to you to comment honestly on the person. Give due praise, but don't overpraise. However, whether to hire the person is not your decision, so avoid an "if I were you . . ." approach.

TIPS

- Be as positive as you can.
- Affirm the desirable qualities of the person about whom you are writing.
- Avoid detrimental comments that may be the basis of later legal action.
- Provide one or two concrete illustrations of the qualities you are endorsing.

Sample 43. Letter of Recommendation I

ABC COMPANY, INC.
123 MAIN STREET
CENTERVILLE, IL 66666

March 15, 19XX

XXXXX X. XXXXXXXXXX
XXXXXXXXXXXX XX.
XXXX XXXXXXXXXX XXX.
XXXXXXXXXX, XX XXXXX

Dear Mr. XXXXXXXXX:

This is to recommend Richard Andrews as an outstanding sales representative.

I've known and worked with Dick for more than ten years. He's always been a self-starter, someone who sniffs out an untapped market and goes for it successfully. For the past few years he has led our sales force in rate of growth.

As you may know, his family situation now calls for him to move outside of our marketing territory. We are very sorry to be losing Dick. We believe that anyone who is fortunate enough to hire him is getting the best there is.

Sincerely,

John P. Rogers
President

amc

Sample 44. Letter of Recommendation II

ABC COMPANY, INC.
123 MAIN STREET
CENTERVILLE, IL 66666

March 15, 19XX

XXXXX X. XXXXXXXXX
XXXXXXXXXXX XX.
XXXX XXXXXXXXX XXX.
XXXXXXXXX, XX XXXXX

Dear Mr. XXXXXXXXX:

Thank you for the opportunity to comment on David Chambley, whom you are considering for the position of head of security.

Mr. Chambley worked for ABC from 19XX to 19XX, steadily rising in responsibility throughout his service with us. He started as a part-time night guard and by 19XX was the assistant security director.

When our former security director retired, we seriously considered Mr. Chambley as his successor. Normally, we would have promoted him. But we had just converted to a major, and highly sensitive, defense-related computer system. Our contract with the federal government called for a person to head security who had at least five years of senior responsibility in computer security controls. Mr. Chambley's experience had been entirely in physical security and therefore he was not eligible for consideration.

We fully sympathize with his seeking a head of security position elsewhere. We have found him to be a person of exceptional integrity. He takes his responsibility very seriously. He works well with his company colleagues, yet makes sure that they adhere to approved security procedures. We are pleased for him that this opportunity has presented itself.

Sincerely,

John P. Rogers
President

JPR:amc

Sample 45. *Letter of Recommendation III*

ABC COMPANY, INC.
123 MAIN STREET
CENTERVILLE, IL 66666

March 15, 19XX

XXXXX X. XXXXXXXXX
XXXXXXXXXXX XX.
XXXX XXXXXXXXX XXX.
XXXXXXXXX, XX XXXXX

Dear Mr. XXXXXXXXX:

You recently requested a letter of recommendation regarding Albert Jones.

Mr. Jones worked for ABC for a period of only eight months, during which period he had an absentee record of three or four sick days a month. As you may know, our company's art department operates under the pressure of meeting deadlines daily for evening television programs. Some people thrive under this kind of pressure. Others do not.

Mr. Jones tried hard to adapt himself to our rather strenuous production deadlines, but did not find it easy to work within our time constraints. His work was of a superior quality, but our needs for continual performance under pressure seemed not to suit his temperament.

When he suggested looking for another position with less constant pressure, we encouraged him to do so. You will see from his portfolio how creative and skilled he is as a designer. If he has the opportunity to work at a more controlled pace, we believe he would be a great asset to a firm.

Sincerely,

John P. Rogers
President

amc

LETTER OF SOLICITATION FOR A GOOD CAUSE

Sometime in a business career, you will have to write a letter seeking contributions to a good cause. You may be the kind of person who seeks out such civic service, and you will not find such a letter difficult to write. Or you may have the responsibility thrust on you, and you would welcome some help in composing an appeal letter.

An appeal letter is much like a sales letter. However, rather than selling a product, you are selling a cause. People give because they approve of the cause, because they are trying to please you, because they will feel better when they give, or because you have touched some chord of emotion or sense of responsibility that they have to respond to. Just as a good sales letter calls for action and makes an immediate response possible, so an appeal letter must call for decision and response right then. If the letter gets set aside for future consideration, chances are it will not be acted on.

TIPS

- Name the cause right at the start and tell why it is important.
- Point out some benefit or sense of fulfillment that the reader will get by giving to the cause.
- Tell the reader of other leaders whom he respects who are contributing to the cause.
- Assure the reader that his contribution will be used to good effect.
- Give a phone number or include a return-addressed, stamped envelope to make it easy for him to respond right then and there.

Sample 46. Letter of Solicitation for a Good Cause I

ABC COMPANY, INC.
123 MAIN STREET
CENTERVILLE, IL 66666

March 15, 19XX

XXXXX X. XXXXXXXXX
XXXXXXXXXXXX XX.
XXXX XXXXXXXXXX XXX.
XXXXXXXXXX, XX XXXXX

Dear Mr. XXXXXXXXX:

The good news is that the Main Street Historical District is now a fact. We all are delighted that the appearance of one of Mid-America's last remaining nineteenth-century industrial centers will be preserved. And we all feel privileged to be working amid such a heritage of earlier achievement.

The Historical District Board has purchased the old McClure factory and is turning it into a museum of nineteenth-century industry. Visitors to Centerville and Centerville schoolchildren will be able to see how our forebears changed America from a mainly rural nation to become the world's industrial giant. The museum will focus on the ingenuity of those pioneer industrialists who paved the way to our own high tech society. The exhibits will be interesting, informative, and inspirational.

The bad news is that the museum is desperately short of funds at a critical time. Right now there are six buildings in the district that are being remodeled inside. If it had the funds, the museum could purchase—at a much reduced cost—priceless artifacts of those early days. It could refurbish them and build much of the beginning exhibit around them. If they are lost now, they are lost forever.

We need $250,000 to take advantage of this unique opportunity. As chairman of the Museum Fund Drive, I'll call you next week to see how your company can help at this critical time. I know your company will want to be listed among the ''Friends of the Museum.''

Sincerely,

John P. Rogers
Chairman, Museum Fund Drive

amc

Sample 47. *Letter of Solicitation for a Good Cause II*

ABC COMPANY, INC.
123 MAIN STREET
CENTERVILLE, IL 66666

March 15, 19XX

XXXXX X. XXXXXXXXXX
XXXXXXXXXXXX XX.
XXXX XXXXXXXXXX XXX.
XXXXXXXXXX, XX XXXXX

Dear Mr. XXXXXXXXX:

Here in Centerville we are fortunate to have the finest library in central Illinois. Our children—indeed all the members of our families—benefit from library services daily.

Right now the Centerville Library faces a crisis. The roof has developed a serious leak and urgently needs repair. The library committee did not plan on this when the budget was adopted this year, so there are no funds available to make the repair.

If 15 businesses in town each gave $500 to the Library Emergency Roof Repair Fund, the need would be met at once. We at ABC Company have started the fund with a donation of $500.

Can I count on you at XXXXX Inc. to contribute also?

Please send your tax deductible contribution to:

>   Roof
>   Centerville Library
>   Box 987
>   Centerville, IL 66666

Help keep our books dry. And thanks.

Sincerely,

John P. Rogers
President

amc

Encl: Self-addressed stamped envelope to "Roof"

CHAPTER 6

Sales Letters

There are two kinds of sales letters. One is the extended letter—together with supporting literature, brochures, order forms, and return envelopes—that is widely used in direct mail sales. This marketing approach is sometimes called "direct response marketing." The intricacies of direct mail letter writing (sometimes called "copy" writing) and packaging are beyond the scope of this book. Readers who want to know more about direct mail sales letter writing are referred to books on direct mail marketing.

The other kind of sales letter is the one you write to an individual. Some of these letters are openers; some are closers. Sales messages can also be included in the routine handling of other questions.

Just as sales lies at the heart of any business enterprise, so sales letters are crucial to a business's continued growth. If new customers are not added or new sales not made to established customers, a business will steadily atrophy. A confident sales focus in letter writing is a sure sign of a vigorous business.

GENERAL SALES LETTER

Every sales letter should include the AIDA factors: A—get the reader's initial *attention;* I—hold his *interest;* D—elicit a *decision;* and A—lead to an *action.* Every time you write a sales letter, ask yourself whether the letter contains each of the four AIDA factors. If it doesn't, strengthen your letter at that point.

The customer will ultimately buy what he wants, not what you want to sell him. Your purpose in writing a sales letter is to show him how what you are selling is what he wants.

TIPS

- Make it very clear to your reader how he will benefit from the service or product that you are writing about.
- Be personal; use the words "you" and "your" in the letter.
- Be clear in your description of the product or service.
- Bring in a reference to someone you both know in common, if suitable.
- Prepare the reader for your future call or visit. This is your sale, so don't leave the initiative entirely to the reader to take the next step.

Sample 48. General Sales Letter I

ABC COMPANY, INC.
123 MAIN STREET
CENTERVILLE, IL 66666

March 15, 19XX

XXXXXXX XX XXXXXXXXXX.
XXXXXXXXXXX
XX XXXXXXX XXX
XXXXXXXXX XX XXXXX

Dear Mr. XXXXXXXXXX:

One proven way to increase sales is to motivate the sales force.

You give your sales force long-range motivation through your commission and bonus policies and through your excellent support system. And, of course, you provide them with first-line products to sell. They take pride in what they sell and in how you back them up.

But now and again a burst of short-range motivation can help some of your fine performers rise to the level of superperformers. Between now and the end of October is your critical time for getting those extra orders that make the difference for the year. Our sales incentive luxury holiday at Montego Bay is just the answer to a flagging sales effort. You choose the winners; we do the rest.

Our Sales Champion Holiday provides for each winner (plus one traveling companion) limousine service to the airport, round-trip first-class air travel, accommodations for three days and four nights in elegant beachside cabanas at Montego Bay's fabulous Hotel Eden, and all meals. The dates to be selected are during January or February 19XX, just that dreary midwinter period when a luxurious break in the Caribbean sun will revitalize your key producers' spirits.

Many businesses have found that such holiday travel incentives are very successful.

May I make an appointment with you next week to demonstrate how little this incentive will cost and how to use it to the maximum effect in getting the results you want?

Sincerely yours,

John P. Rogers
President

amc

Sample 49. General Sales Letter II

CENTERVILLE SWIM CENTER
456 BROAD STREET
CENTERVILLE, IL 66666

March 15, 19XX

XXXXXXX XX XXXXXXXXXX
XXXXXXXXXXX
XX XXXXXXX XXX
XXXXXXXXX XX XXXXX

Dear Mr. XXXXXXXXXX:

Your health is your greatest asset. Protect it and enhance it. And you'll feel better for doing so.

One of the essentials of good health is regular exercise. But one of the most boring methods of getting exercise is doing push-ups and sit-ups and bend-overs. How many times have you told yourself that you'll take care of yourself, only to see that fine resolution fade after a week of dull routine.

We have the answer you are looking for. Swimming is the best all-around exercise there is. Every muscle in your body moves against the resistance of the water. Whether your swimming is recreational and relaxing or vigorous and competitive, you treat your body to the exercise it needs. In addition, swimming is an aerobic activity—one that fills your lungs with air and your blood with oxygen.

Come swim with us. Before you go to work. During your lunch break. After work is done. In the quiet of the evening. Two or three swims a week will enhance your health, improve your mental outlook, increase your zest for life.

We have annual memberships, short-term memberships, and inexpensive guest privileges. After your swim, relax in our sun room; enjoy our sauna and steam room. All our facilities are shared by men and women. Our snack and salad bar is always open.

You'll like our rates. You'll love our facilities. And you'll live on a higher level of health and vitality. Come and try a free week of swimming.

Just bring this letter in with you to sign up for your free week of swimming for you and your guest.

Sincerely,

Robert M. Young
Director

RMY/pat

SALES LETTER TO AN INACTIVE CUSTOMER

Inactive customers once bought your products or services. For some reason they no longer do. It may be because the customer is upset with your company, your product or service, or some member of your staff for some reason. It may be that the customer no longer has need of your product or service, but still feels positive about your company. Or it may be that some competitor was able to win the customer's business away from you by selling a better product or more service or greater "sizzle." Your letter is aimed to unearth any grievance, resell your company, and introduce any new products or services that can win your customer back.

TIPS

- Assure the customer that you have always thought him to be a valued customer and that you still think of him in that light.
- Ask why the customer no longer does business with you.
- Assure the customer that you would like to regain his business.
- Tell the customer that your products or services are better than ever and that you have every confidence that he will find doing business with you to his complete satisfaction.

Sample 50. Sales Letter to an Inactive Customer I

ABC COMPANY, INC.
123 MAIN STREET
CENTERVILLE, IL 66666

March 15, 19XX

XXXXXXX XX XXXXXXXXXX
XXXXXXXXXXX
XX XXXXXXX XXX
XXXXXXXXX XX XXXXX

Dear Mr. XXXXXXXXXX:

Have we done something wrong?

We have missed serving you over the past ten months. Up until then we counted you among our steadiest customers. We were confident that we were serving you with quiet efficiency and with quality products. Every two or three months your order came in—and was generally filled overnight.

When your orders ceased, we thought it was a delay in your ordering cycle. Now we wonder whether some failure on our part has caused you to seek service elsewhere. We know that with our improved fulfillment procedure and our larger warehouse that we can provide a greater variety of products and quicker response than was true even six months ago.

We want your business. We know we can serve you well. Please let me know personally what we can do to reestablish our relationship with you once again.

Sincerely yours,

Mark L. Cannon
Marketing Manager

MLC:wn

Sample 51. Sales Letter to an Inactive Customer II

CENTERVILLE SWIM CENTER
456 BROAD STREET
CENTERVILLE, IL 66666

March 15, 19XX

XXXXXXX XX XXXXXXXXXX
XXXXXXXXXXX
XX XXXXXXX XXX
XXXXXXXXX XX XXXXX

Dear Mr. XXXXXXXXXX:

It's hard for us to imagine that it's been ten months since we last saw you at the Swim Center.

Four years ago you took out a short-term membership. Then you renewed your membership for two years running—and our records show that you came regularly. Obviously, we were meeting your needs.

Now you are among the missing. And we'd love to see you again.

We do have a special renewal offer in effect during this month. A form with the rates—together with a description of our remodeled sauna facilities—is enclosed for your use. When we first opened, we made a pledge to our members (and ourselves) to improve the Swim Center each year of operation. We believe you get better value for your membership now than when you first joined. And it will be even better during this coming year.

We miss you and hope to see you in the very near future.

Sincerely,

Robert M. Young
Director

RMY/pat

INTRODUCTION TO A REQUEST FOR A DEMONSTRATION OR INTERVIEW

When you write ahead about making a demonstration or having an interview, make your letter do more than just set up the time and place. Use your letter to sell: sell your product, your company, your service, yourself. Word your letter in such a way that your proposed customer will look forward to meeting and hearing what you have to say.

TIPS

- Be brief. Write to the point.
- Tell enough to whet the reader's appetite. But don't tell so much that he no longer believes he needs to give you the interview.
- Try to make the appointment firm. Indicate you will call to confirm it.

Sample 52. Introduction to a Request for a Demonstration or Interview I

ABC COMPANY, INC.
123 MAIN STREET
CENTERVILLE, IL 66666

March 15, 19XX

XXXXXX XX XXXXXXXXX
XXXXXXXXXX
XX XXXXXXX XXX
XXXXXXXX XX XXXXX

Dear Mr. XXXXXXXXX:

As an ABC Personal Computer user, you have learned how rich a range of functions it performs.

Now we can offer you a high-speed <u>laser printer</u> that gives your work the appearance of expensive typeset copy. Think how much you can save on printing jobs. Letters, manuals, instructions, catalogs, price lists—all can be printed directly by your ABC PC.

Would you kindly give me thirty minutes to show you the versatility of this new printer to do the work you need done. I will call you at the beginning of next week to set up a mutually convenient appointment.

Sincerely yours,

Harold J. Winston
Regional Representative

HJW:sh

Sample 53. *Introduction to a Request for a Demonstration or Interview II*

ABC COMPANY, INC.
123 MAIN STREET
CENTERVILLE, IL 66666

March 15, 19XX

XXXXXXX XX XXXXXXXXXX
XXXXXXXXXXX
XX XXXXXXX XXX
XXXXXXXXX XX XXXXX

Dear Mr. XXXXXXXXX:

Your success in life can be measured by many yardsticks.

A fine Mercedes-Benz or Cadillac automobile is one such yardstick. And driving such a car can be far less costly than most people imagine.

Our new Execu-Lease program for business leaders may be just the right program for you. We have new rates, new length of lease arrangements, new insurance and maintenance services, and new executive automobiles—designed to put you behind the wheel of an elegant, luxurious car at a cost so low you won't believe it at first.

May I drop by your office for a few minutes next week to give you a test drive and to explain how our Execu—Lease program works? In order to know which kind of car you'd like to test drive, I'll call you in a couple of days to make arrangements.

Looking forward to seeing you, I am

Yours sincerely,

Peter L. Kinnon
Execu—Lease Division

PLK/rc

FOLLOW-UP AFTER A DEMONSTRATION OR INTERVIEW

A letter that follows up a demonstration you have made or an interview that has been granted to you builds on the foundation already laid. It permits you to thank the person for the sale or to remind him again of the value of your service or product. It also makes him feel positive about you and your company. Since sending a follow-up letter shows him that you are thorough in your presentation, it may also convince him that your company will be thorough in providing the product or service support he looks for.

TIPS

- Thank the person for giving you the time for the interview or for the opportunity of making the demonstration.
- Review one or two main selling points. It is better to reinforce one point you recall he was impressed with than to introduce new selling points that you forgot to make at the demonstration or have thought of since.
- Be enthusiastic about his business and about the opportunity you have of doing business with his company.

Sample 54. Follow-up After a Demonstration or Interview I

ABC COMPANY, INC.
123 MAIN STREET
CENTERVILLE, IL 66666

March 15, 19XX

XXXXXXX XX XXXXXXXXXX
XXXXXXXXXXX
XX XXXXXXX XXX
XXXXXXXXX XX XXXXX

Dear Mr. XXXXXXXXXX:

Many thanks for giving me an hour last week to demonstrate our new laser printer. I realize how tight your time was in the light of your trip the next day to Washington, so I am doubly appreciative.

I was pleased that you saw so quickly how the laser printer could solve your need for "instant" price lists in a setting where your costs are so volatile.

I have taken the liberty of preparing a printing format based on the copy you gave me of your present price list. Once the prices are changed in your ABC PC, you can have those fifty copies of the price list we talked about in only five minutes. That's quite a contrast to the two or three days you said it normally takes to get them typeset.

I'd also like to reemphasize that part of our support service includes assisting your people develop printing formats for your major repetitive needs. If I read Joe Tidwell's interest right, it won't be long before he is helping us solve some difficult formatting problems!

Our analysis of your figures shows that you can pay for the printer with eighteen months of typesetter's charges, not counting the great savings in time and work duplication. Please let me know if there is any more information you need to come to a decision.

Looking forward to being of service to you, I am

Yours sincerely,

Harold J. Winston
Regional Representative

HJW:sh

Sample 55. Follow-up After a Demonstration or Interview II

ABC COMPANY, INC.
123 MAIN STREET
CENTERVILLE, IL 66666

March 15, 19XX

XXXXXXX XX XXXXXXXXXX
XXXXXXXXXXX
XX XXXXXXX XXX
XXXXXXXXX XX XXXXX

Dear Mr. XXXXXXXXXX:

It was such a pleasure meeting you. I know how much you enjoyed driving around town in our latest model convertible.

You asked about the Execu—Lease program for a large four—door sedan. The enclosed sheet gives you all the information you requested. Delivery can be made within two weeks of our receiving your order; usually, we can make same—day delivery, especially if we have a couple of days' advance notice that you will be placing the order.

May I call you next Thursday—hopefully to take your order for the new car you want?

With all good wishes, I remain

Sincerely yours,

Peter L. Kinnon
Execu—Lease.Division

PLK/rc

A GENERAL MORALE BUILDER FOR SALESPEOPLE

Even though sales people are generally gregarious and optimistic, they are often physically alone in their territory and psychologically alone in having to face new, unknown prospects. A letter that encourages them both reassures them and spurs them to increased effort. It is an inexpensive way of underlining your belief in them and stressing their importance to the growth of the company.

TIPS

- Stress the key role that the sales force plays in the life of the company.
- Thank them for what they have achieved so far this year; hold out to them the goals that are as yet unreached.

- Make a positive suggestion on some particular way in which sales improvement can be made.
- Without making the letter into a newsletter, give some news item about someone or some event related to sales that will serve as good news.

Sample 56. A General Morale Builder to Salespeople I

ABC COMPANY, INC.
123 MAIN STREET
CENTERVILLE, IL 66666

October 15, 19XX

XXXXXXX XX XXXXXXXXX
XXXXXXXXXXX
XX XXXXXXX XXX
XXXXXXXXX XX XXXXX

Dear XXXXXXXXXX:

Final sales figures for 19XX are in.

You made the top 5 percent of sales performers this year. In fact, you personally brought in 16.8 percent of our total sales. My warmest congratulations to you for such an outstanding performance. This splendid record will, of course, be financially recognized when bonuses are distributed in December.

I also note that during the first quarter of this fiscal year you are running ahead of last year's sales. It is especially gratifying to see that this is based on getting three new major accounts, as well as improving on our regular accounts. It is because of the initiative and drive of salespeople like you that ABC is itself becoming an industry leader.

We have some exciting new products in R & D that are in the beta test stage now and should be in your product bag early next year. With the combination of your enthusiasm and sales skills and the company's industry recognition for product innovation, we should all have the best year ever just before us.

Congratulations again for your fine record during the year just past. I expect I'll have to invent new words to express the company's thanks for this year when the final results are in.

Sincerely,

John P. Rogers
President

amc

Sample 57. A General Morale Builder for Salespeople II

ABC COMPANY, INC.
123 MAIN STREET
CENTERVILLE, IL 66666

March 15, 19XX

XXXXXXX XX XXXXXXXXXX
XXXXXXXXXXX
XX XXXXXXX XXX
XXXXXXXXX XX XXXXX

Dear XXXXXXXXXX:

So many times when the boss writes a letter, it's because there's a problem that has to be faced. Not so with this letter.

I've just been thinking over the people in the company who are essential to its success and future. You came immediately to mind. Sales are the lifeblood of every commercial enterprise. Your commitment to the company, your knowledge of its products and services, your drive and ambition to be a leading salesperson, and your energy and wide range of industry contacts have all combined to make your contribution to ABC an outstanding one.

I look forward to continuing to work with you during the years ahead as together we strive to make our company the industry leader.

Sincerely,

John P. Rogers
President

amc

INTRODUCING A NEW SALESPERSON

A letter of introduction to established customers will make it much easier for a new salesperson during that first visit. Your customer will be flattered that you thought enough of him to let him know personally of a change in your staff that affects him.

TIPS

- Be personal in your letter—friend introducing friend to friend.
- Provide enough information about your new representative to impress your customer positively, but not so much as to intimidate him.
- Show confidence in the ability of your new representative to serve the customer with satisfaction.

Sample 58. Introducing a New Salesperson I

ABC COMPANY, INC.
123 MAIN STREET
CENTERVILLE, IL 66666

March 15, 19XX

XXXXXXX XX XXXXXXXXXX
XXXXXXXXXXX
XX XXXXXXX XXX
XXXXXXXXX XX XXXXX

Dear Mr. XXXXXXXXXX:

We are pleased indeed to introduce John V. McMannion, our new field
representative for the tri-state area.

John comes to us with an outstanding record in the paper industry. More than
most salespeople, he knows the business from the plant up. He "apprenticed" in
the mills in New England and Minnesota, learning every step in the making of
fine paper. He later served as a "journeyman" by working in the quality book
printing industry, seeing paper in use. He especially worked with superthin
opaque paper—less than 20#—used in dictionary, encyclopedia, and Bible work.
Now he is in the early stages of his "master" period. He is fully qualified to
assist you in determining just the right paper to meet each of your job needs.

I know you'll like John as a person. I'm confident you'll respect him as a
professional. I hope you'll come to regard John as a friend as he finds
opportunity to serve you in your exacting work.

With much appreciation for our long-standing relationship, I remain

Yours sincerely,

John P. Rogers
President

amc

Sample 59. Introducing a New Salesperson II

ABC COMPANY, INC.
123 Main Street
Centerville, IL 66666

March 15, 19XX

XXXXXXX XX XXXXXXXXXX
XXXXXXXXXXX
XX XXXXXXX XXX
XXXXXXXXX XX XXXXX

Dear Mr. XXXXXXXXXX:

I wish I could introduce Marg Johnson to you personally. This letter will have
to serve instead.

Marg was recently brought onto our staff as a communications analyst and
consultant for your region. Her job is to make your communications and
information systems work better and easier, with less problems. She knows
communications well—with an advanced degree in the field. More important, she
knows it in a practical way; she was the MIS manager at Intrabank.

Marg knows our equipment and software well. She will call on you as new
equipment comes into line that may enhance your communications capabilities.
And be sure to call on Marg whenever you have a communications question.

Sincerely,

Warren R. Peters
Mid—central District Manager

WRP:jb

ANSWERING A REQUEST FOR INFORMATION

A routine request from a customer or a potential customer offers an opportunity to sell a
product or service. The fact that the person is sufficiently interested to write in the first place
or to fill out a customer service card indicates that your company or the product/service is
very much in the customer's mind. You often have to work hard to find a good lead; here
one comes to you.

TIPS

- Be sure to thank the writer for the inquiry.
- Answer the person's question directly. It can be very frustrating to ask a specific question

but receive a letter that does not deal with the question. Save the expensive color sales brochures for a follow-up letter or a representative's follow-up visit.
* Ask the inquirer to feel free to seek any further information he might want.

Sample 60. Answering a Request for Information I

ABC COMPANY, INC.
123 MAIN STREET
CENTERVILLE, IL 66666

March 15, 19XX

XXXXXXX XX XXXXXXXXXX
XXXXXXXXXXX
XX XXXXXXX XXX
XXXXXXXXX XX XXXXX

Dear Mrs. XXXXXXXXXX:

Thank you for your request for information concerning our small quilting frame.

This quilting frame measures two by three feet and stands at a height that is convenient to work on as you sit on a sofa or in an easy chair. It comes in easy-to-assemble parts, together with clear, illustrated directions on assembly and use. The frame costs $24.50, plus $4.50 handling and shipping charges, or a total of $29.00. Payment can be made by check or money order, or call us with credit card information. Since you do not live in Illinois, no state sales tax is required.

After having bought a quilting frame for their own use, hundreds of our frame customers have recommended our frame to their friends. This kind of word-of-mouth advertising is very satisfying to us and speaks well of the product. We know you will be very happy with the increased convenience in quilting that our frame provides.

Hoping to receive your order soon, I am

Yours sincerely,

Mary S. Hopkins
National Service

MSH:bm

Sample 61. Answering a Request for Information II

ABC COMPANY, INC.
123 MAIN STREET
CENTERVILLE, IL 66666

March 15, 19XX

XXXXXXX XX XXXXXXXXXX
XXXXXXXXXXX
XX XXXXXXX XXX
XXXXXXXXX XX XXXXX

Dear Mr. XXXXXXXXXX:

Thank you so much for your inquiry about our office copier. Under separate cover
I am sending an illustrated brochure that explains the features of several
models.

We have learned over the years that we cannot guess at a customer's needs and the
applications he would make of an office copier. We have found it works best to
have one of our representatives call on you to discuss your copying needs and
only then to suggest one or two models that would meet those needs.

Harry Reynolds, our representative who serves your city, will call to make an
appointment. When he calls, he will ask some preliminary questions to prepare
himself to show you the best copier for your situation.

We pride ourselves that our quality copier is only half of the story. Our
service and supply support is the other half. If you ever have down time, we will
adjust our service priorities to match your needs.

Thank you again for your inquiry. We look forward to the possibility of serving
you for years to come.

Sincerely,

Thomas K. O'Neill
Marketing Director

bm

FOLLOW-UP SALES LETTER

A possible sales lead is a person who drops by your booth at an exhibition, someone you
meet at a trade convention, or a person who has requested your company's literature. Rather
than allow that brief show of interest to wither without any response from you, a follow-up
letter may be a major factor in converting the person's general interest into a sale.

TIPS

- Tell the person at the start why you are writing.
- Thank the person for the interest that has been shown.
- In a short paragraph, tell what you are basically about.
- Offer further information.
- Introduce a representative who will call on the person at a later date.

Sample 62. Follow-up Sales Letter I

ABC COMPANY, INC.
123 MAIN STREET
CENTERVILLE, IL 66666

March 15, 19XX

XXXXXXX XX XXXXXXXXXX
XXXXXXXXXXX
XX XXXXXXX XXX
XXXXXXXXX XX XXXXX

Dear Mr. XXXXXXXXXX:

It was very pleasant meeting you at our booth at the trade exhibition last week. I was most interested to hear how you have used your data and word processing computers to speed your typesetting through coding and communications. You are certainly far ahead of most companies in this dramatic application of the technology.

I was sorry that you didn't have the time to see our page-makeup software in a demonstration. We have a program that is machine-specific to your equipment. It will enable you to perform typesetting functions on your microcomputer, including choosing a particular typeface, performing hyphenation/ justification, setting point sizes and leading, setting measures in picas, and seeing on your screen just how each line will break and how that page will look.

We suggest that you write, edit, and finalize the content of your copy on your word processing program, and <u>then</u> shape it for type with our software. You will be astounded at how easy this task now is and how quickly it can be done.

May I call you next week to set up a demonstration in your office?

I look forward to seeing you again then.

Sincerely yours,

Thomas K. O'Neill
Marketing Director

bm

Sample 63. Follow-up Sales Letter II

ABC COMPANY, INC.
123 MAIN STREET
CENTERVILLE, IL 66666

March 15, 19XX

XXXXXXX XX XXXXXXXXXX
XXXXXXXXXXX
XX XXXXXXX XXX
XXXXXXXXX XX XXXXX

Dear Mr. XXXXXXXXXX:

Thank you for leaving your card with our receptionist at the trade convention last week. I'm sorry none of our staff were available right then to meet with you.

According to Miss Jones, the young woman who took your card, you wanted to know something about typesetting software for office computers. We will be most pleased to provide any information we can that will be of help to you.

Under separate cover I am sending you a general description of our typesetting/microcomputer programs. More importantly, I have asked Ken Roundtree, our eastern marketing representative, to call you to find out more about your specific applications. When we know what you are doing in this field, or what you hope to do, we can focus far more helpfully on that particular program that best would meet your need. Then Ken would like to set up a demonstration in your office, so you can give the package a realistic hands-on trial to see if it really does make your work easier.

Again, we're sorry to have missed you personally. But we're glad we didn't miss you altogether. Thanks for your expression of interest. We hope your needs and our program mesh to our mutual benefit.

Sincerely,

Thomas K. O'Neill
Marketing Director

bm

STAY-IN-TOUCH LETTER

There are sometimes good reasons to remind your customers that you are still there and that you are continually working at upgrading the level of your service and products. One way to remind them and at the same time secure feedback from them is to send them a short questionnaire. Always include a self-addressed envelope or print the questionnaire on a business reply card, making it easy for them to fill out the form and send it to you. The questionnaire or survey shows you are committed to knowing your market and to improving your business.

TIPS

- Explain the purpose of the questionnaire or survey.
- Tell how responding will help you to help the reader.
- Thank the reader for filling in the survey and returning it.

Sample 64. Stay-in-Touch Letter I

ABC COMPANY, INC.
123 MAIN STREET
CENTERVILLE, IL 66666

March 15, 19XX

XXXXXXX XX XXXXXXXXXX
XXXXXXXXXXX
XX XXXXXXX XXX
XXXXXXXXX XX XXXXX

Dear Mr. XXXXXXXXXX:

"How are we doin'?" to borrow a phrase from a famous mayor.

We'd like you to tell us how <u>you</u> think we're doing. We value your opinion—indeed, your opinion is vital to the growth and success of our company. If you don't like what we're doing or how we're doing it, our business is in trouble.

Please fill in the enclosed short questionnaire and return it to us in the self-addressed, stamped envelope. We would especially benefit from any comments you wish to write about your experience with us and our service. We always like to hear good things (that shows we're doing it right)—and we need to hear not so good things (that tells us where we need to improve).

Thank you very much for your help.

Sincerely,

Thomas K. O'Neill
Marketing Director

bm

Sample 65. Stay-in-Touch Letter II

ABC COMPANY, INC.
123 MAIN STREET
CENTERVILLE, IL 66666

March 15, 19XX

XXXXXXX XX XXXXXXXXXX
XXXXXXXXXXX
XX XXXXXXX XXX
XXXXXXXXX XX XXXXX

Dear Mr. XXXXXXXXXX:

ABC Hot-Line is renowned throughout the trade as the most reliable, most up-to-date, and most readable newsletter for busy executives.

We are pleased to send it every other month without cost to people who count in the industry. We think you benefit in some practical way every time you leaf through a copy.

But we need to know what you think—in order to make sure your interests are covered. We need to know what you are doing now, since people in our industry move ahead so rapidly. And we need to confirm that our address for you is still the right one.

In order to continue on our free ABC Hot-Line mailing list, please fill out and return the enclosed questionnaire. Just initial it after checking the appropriate boxes and drop it in the mail. Any written comments are especially appreciated.

Many thanks, and we hope to stay in touch with you,

Sincerely,

Thomas K. O'Neill
Marketing Director

bm

WHEN A CUSTOMER HAS BEEN PROMOTED OR HAS CHANGED JOBS

It is easier to keep an old customer than to win a new customer. If your business is directed to individuals as well as to businesses as such, you can continue to have the patronage of a person who changes jobs. A letter of congratulations and good wishes builds continued goodwill toward your company.

When you learn of the promotion of one of your customers, a letter of congratulations will be long remembered.

TIPS

- Be positive about the change of job or promotion.
- Extend good wishes.
- Indicate that you hope to continue to be of service in this new circumstance.

Sample 66. When a Customer Has Been Promoted or Has Changed Jobs I

ABC COMPANY, INC.
123 MAIN STREET
CENTERVILLE, IL 66666

March 15, 19XX

XXXXXXX XX XXXXXXXXXX
XXXXXXXXXXX
XX XXXXXXX XXX
XXXXXXXXX XX XXXXX

Dear Mr. XXXXXXXXXX:

I hear that congratulations are in order!

Your promotion to national marketing manager certainly came as no surprise to us. We have seen the drive and success you brought to the regional sales manager position here in the Central Region, and we knew that in time you would be tapped for a headquarters assignment.

You came to know us and our service well during the past four years, and you know that we stand ready to be of continued service to you in the days ahead.

We extend every good wish to you in this challenging task.

Sincerely yours,

John P. Rogers
President

amc

Sample 67. When a Customer Has Been Promoted or Has Changed Jobs II

ABC COMPANY, INC.
123 MAIN STREET
CENTERVILLE, IL 66666

March 15, 19XX

XXXXXX XX XXXXXXXXX
XXXXXXXXXX
XX XXXXXX XXX
XXXXXXXX XX XXXXX

Dear XXXXXXXXX:

The grapevine news reports that you have left the XYZ Corporation to take on a new challenge at MNO, Ltd. Congratulations on this fine opportunity.

In our industry—like most, I guess—reputations develop about people, based on the work they do and the way they do it. You should be pleased to know that your fine reputation follows you to MNO, bearing the highest of respect from all your industry colleagues. We don't know who's the luckier about this move, you or MNO; we do know they are fortunate getting you at this time.

We have always appreciated the thoughtful, professional dealings we have had with you. And we hope it will be possible to develop these relations with you at MNO. Do let us know when and how we can be of service.

With every good wish to you in this new venture, I am

Yours sincerely,

John P. Rogers
President

amc

WHEN A CUSTOMER IS ILL OR INJURED

Time hangs heavy for busy people when they are sick. A letter written to a customer who is ill or injured is sure to create long-lasting goodwill. If you can also send something of interest to read, the customer will realize that you have given him special thought and will even more appreciate your getting in touch.

TIPS

- Be brief.
- Depending on how well you know the person, be personal without overfamiliarity.
- If there is still some question about the outcome, don't joke. But don't be solemn, either.
- Send along something of interest for the person to read.

Sample 68. When a Customer Is Ill or Injured I

ABC COMPANY, INC.
123 MAIN STREET
CENTERVILLE, IL 66666

March 15, 19XX

XXXXXXX XX XXXXXXXXXX
XXXXXXXXXXX
XX XXXXXXX XXX
XXXXXXXXX XX XXXXX

Dear Mr. XXXXXXXXXX:

I only now learned that you are in the hospital recovering from bypass surgery. Even though they say the operation is "routine" these days, I know it hardly seemed "routine" to you!

I'm glad that the operation was a success and that you are reported well on the way to recovery. You must find the restrictions of hospital life a bore, but do your best to get as much rest as you can while you are there. Just to keep your hand in, I'm enclosing the latest copy of Micro Update, which has an in-depth assessment of the Model 759 that you recently purchased from us. You can dream up some new things to do with it while you stare at the ceiling!

We all look forward to seeing you back on the job again in a short while.

Regards, as ever,

John P. Rogers
President

amc

Sample 69. When a Customer Is Ill or Injured II

ABC COMPANY, INC.
123 MAIN STREET
CENTERVILLE, IL 66666

March 15, 19XX

XXXXXXX XX XXXXXXXXXX
XXXXXXXXXXX
XX XXXXXXX XXX
XXXXXXXXX XX XXXXX

Dear XXXXXXXXXX:

I just now heard about the accident.

It was such a relief to learn that you came out of it with relatively minor
damage even though your car was completely totaled. (I know you could argue with
me about that "minor" bit.) You'll have to tell me all about how it happened when
we see each other next.

I recently read a fascinating book about artificial intelligence and expert
systems. Knowing your interest in this area, I'm sending my copy to you under
separate cover. Please ignore my comments in the margins. Or if you can't ignore
them, tell me what you think of them and the subject when you finish. I want the
book back in time, but there's no rush at all on it.

Get well. Mend quickly and completely. And get back to work! Doing business at
XYZ is just not the same with your being away.

Please give Roberta my regards.

Sincerely,

John P. Rogers
President

amc

WHEN THERE IS A DEATH IN A CUSTOMER'S FAMILY

A letter of sympathy—with no sales message—is appropriate when you learn that a close member of a customer's family has just died. In such a letter, avoid philosophizing or moralizing. It is enough to tell the customer that you are thinking of him during this time of sorrow.

TIPS

- Be brief.
- You cannot know exactly how the person feels, so avoid telling him you do. You can, however, share a similar kind of experience that you may have had, without making it say too much.
- Be only as personal as your friendship permits, but be personal to that extent.
- Extend condolences on behalf of the company, if appropriate, and extend condolences to the family, even if you do not know them.

Sample 70. When There Is a Death in a Customer's Family I

ABC COMPANY, INC.
123 MAIN STREET
CENTERVILLE, IL 66666

March 15, 19XX

XXXXXXX XX XXXXXXXXXX
XXXXXXXXXXX
XX XXXXXXX XXX
XXXXXXXXX XX XXXXX

Dear Mr. XXXXXXXXXX:

I just learned of your mother's death. Please accept my sympathy at this time of family sorrow.

Having lost my own mother last year, I am close enough to the event to remember the pain of the loss and the regrets for all those things I wish could have been otherwise. This is a time of very special loss for you, and I just wanted you to know you are in our thoughts.

Please extend our condolences to the members of your family.

Sincerely,

John P. Rogers
President

amc

Sample 71. When There Is a Death in a Customer's Family II

ABC COMPANY, INC.
123 MAIN STREET
CENTERVILLE, IL 66666

March 15, 19XX

XXXXXXX XX XXXXXXXXXX
XXXXXXXXXXX
XX XXXXXXX XXX
XXXXXXXXX XX XXXXX

Dear XXXXXXXXXX:

It was such a shock to learn that Debbie was killed in a car accident over the
weekend.

I know that even though you are going through the motions, you must be utterly
numb. She was such a beautiful young woman and had such a vibrant love of living
each day to the full.

I can't offer a word to help soften your pain. I only want you to know that you
and your family are very much in my thoughts.

With sorrow and concern, I remain

Sincerely,

John P. Rogers
President

amc

WHEN SOMETHING GOOD HAPPENS IN A CUSTOMER'S LIFE

When a customer's son or daughter is married or a grandchild is born, a letter of congratulations is a goodwill builder. You do not sell anything directly in this kind of letter; but you
do create an atmosphere wherein it is much easier to do business in the future. This kind of
letter does not *have* to be written, but if it is written, it is well worth the effort in the long
run.

TIPS

- Be brief.
- Be personal.
- Make your letter happy in tone.

Sample 72. When Something Good Happens in a Customer's Life I

ABC COMPANY, INC.
123 MAIN STREET
CENTERVILLE, IL 66666

March 15, 19XX

XXXXXXX XX XXXXXXXXX
XXXXXXXXXXX
XX XXXXXXX XXX
XXXXXXXXX XX XXXXX

Dear XXXXXXXXXX:

I hear that your first grandchild just arrived safely and well. That's great news!

If you dote on yours only half as much as we dote on ours, you'll be insufferable. But then, that's a grandparent's privilege.

The other thing you will discover is how much more expensive children's clothing has become since those days twenty-five years ago when you bought for Maxine. We never even had the option of buying designer diapers in those far-off days.

I know this first grandchild will bring you much joy during the years to come.

With good wishes,

Sincerely,

John P. Rogers
President

amc

Sample 73. When Something Good Happens in a Customer's Life II

ABC COMPANY, INC.
123 MAIN STREET
CENTERVILLE, IL 66666

March 15, 19XX

XXXXXXX XX XXXXXXXXX
XXXXXXXXXXX
XX XXXXXXX XXX
XXXXXXXXX XX XXXXX

Dear Mr. XXXXXXXXXX:

When I called you at the office the other day, your assistant told me that you
were away because your son was getting married that afternoon in Muncie. What a
happy occasion it must have been for you and your family.

When my son got married, I remember I was almost as nervous as he was. He looked
so <u>young</u> to be taking on such responsibility. And then I remembered that he was
four years older than I was when I got married.

You'll have to show me pictures of the wedding when we see each other next month
at the convention.

Regards,

John P. Rogers
President

amc

WHEN YOU READ ABOUT A CUSTOMER

You may read about a customer in the local newspaper or in a trade publication. You do
not know whether your customer has seen the article. He will greatly value a letter from you
that commends him on the appearance of the article. You might enclose a clipping or a photocopy of the article. If the article deals with your business field, you might also use the article
as a springboard to discuss further business possibilities.

TIPS

- Be personal.
- Send a clipping or a photocopy of the article.
- Give congratulations if the article is about some achievement.
- Use the opportunity to suggest a further business development that arises out of the
  subject covered in the article, if appropriate.

Sample 74. When You Read About a Customer I

ABC COMPANY, INC.
123 MAIN STREET
CENTERVILLE, IL 66666

March 15, 19XX

XXXXXXX XX XXXXXXXXX
XXXXXXXXXXX
XX XXXXXXX XXX
XXXXXXXXX XX XXXXX

Dear Mr. XXXXXXXXXX:

What a pleasant surprise yesterday to see your photograph in the Herald. The story on the new wing at the hospital and the leadership you are giving to the fund-raising drive was most interesting and impressive.

I have always admired your civic commitment. A public contribution of this nature will benefit hundreds of Centervillians each year for scores of years to come. On behalf of your friends at ABC, I want to extend our "Well done."

With every hope that the drive will soon go over the top and construction can begin,

Sincerely,

John P. Rogers
President

amc

Sample 75. When You Read About a Customer II

ABC COMPANY, INC.
123 MAIN STREET
CENTERVILLE, IL 66666

March 15, 19XX

XXXXXXX XX XXXXXXXXX
XXXXXXXXXXX
XX XXXXXXX XXX
XXXXXXXXX XX XXXXX

Dear XXXXXXXXXX:

I don't know whether you read the March issue of <u>Micro</u> <u>Update</u>.

In case you missed it, here's a clipping from the issue that tells about your
experimental use of portable PCs by your sales force. I thought it was
fascinating the way you use telecommunications right in the customer's presence
to get an up-to-the-second inventory status report and to place the order into
your main system in "real time" right then and there.

I <u>know</u> this use is more efficient. I imagine it really wows the customer.

This report got me to thinking about other uses of the portable that could be
made by a decentralized sales force. Let's have lunch soon and talk about it.

Sincerely,

John P. Rogers
President

amc

CHAPTER 7

Credit and Collection Letters

Effective sales letters create sales. But unfortunately not all customers pay their accounts promptly. The problem is so widespread that larger corporations have entire departments that are dedicated to credit and collection activities. Letters written to secure payment of an overdue bill, but designed to retain customer loyalty, are difficult to write.

Some customers need only a polite reminder. Others may be having cash flow problems and, therefore, need several letters that increasingly become more firm. And a few may respond only to a threat of some kind of legal action.

There are a number of character traits to which you can appeal to motivate your customer to make payment. One is an appeal to fairness—you have to run your business, too. This is an indirect appeal to his sense of pride—you don't expect him to let you down. There is also an appeal to his self-interest—it would be to his benefit to pay lest something undesirable happen.

Before granting credit to a potential customer, you may wish to conduct a credit check on the customer. Whether you do so depends on the nature of your business and the amount of the sale.

CREDIT INQUIRY LETTER

Your customer may be a business or an individual. You can secure business references from the business or person who wishes you to extend credit or to open an account.

TIPS

- Make this a short, direct letter. Do not give unnecessary information about the proposed customer.
- Ask for the information you want with a brief explanation of why you want it.
- Offer to assist in like manner anytime in the future.
- Stress that the confidentiality of any information will be honored.
- Since you are asking for a business favor, enclose a SASE as a courtesy.

Sample 76. Credit Inquiry Letter I

ABC COMPANY, INC.
123 MAIN STREET
CENTERVILLE, IL 66666

March 15, 19XX

Credit Manager
XXXXXXXXXX
XX XXXXXX XXX
XXXXXXXX XX XXXXX

MNO, Ltd., of Peoria has given the name of your firm to us as a reference. MNO
wishes to establish an account with us with estimated purchases in the low four
figures monthly.

Any information you can give us that would assist us in making a judicious
decision would be much appreciated. It will, of course, be held in strict
confidence.

Be assured of our appreciation for your assistance and of our willingness to
extend such information to you whenever needed.

Sincerely,

John D. Lamont
Credit Manager

JDL/jk

Sample 77. Credit Inquiry Letter II

ABC COMPANY, INC.
123 MAIN STREET
CENTERVILLE, IL 66666

March 15, 19XX

Credit Manager
XXXXXXXXXX
XX XXXXXX XXX
XXXXXXXX XX XXXXX

Mr. John Doe, of 1313 Z Street, Peoria, IL 61601, has applied for an account with
our company. He listed you as a reference in his application.

We would be most grateful for any information you can give us about Mr. Doe's creditworthiness and reputation that will help us in making a decision about his application.

Any information you send us will be held in strict confidence. Since Mr. Doe wishes an early decision from us, we would be extra grateful for an early comment. A reply envelope is enclosed.

Thank you for help in this matter. Please let us know if we can ever be of like assistance.

Sincerely yours,

John D. Lamont
Credit Manager

JDL/jk

GRANTING CREDIT

Your pleasure in finding a customer who appears to be a good credit risk should show itself in this letter. Avoid overstating your pleasure, but make it a happy letter.

TIPS

- Tell the person that you contacted his references, if in fact you actually did so.
- Set whatever terms you wish to the extension of credit.
- Welcome the person or company as a customer with pleasure.

Sample 78. Granting Credit I

ABC COMPANY, INC.
123 MAIN STREET
CENTERVILLE, IL 66666

March 15, 19XX

XX XXXXXX XX XXXXXXX
XXXXXXXXXXX
XX XXXXXXX XXX
XXXXXXXXX XX XXXXX

Dear Mr. XXXXXXX:

We are very pleased to welcome you as a customer. The references you gave us provided most satisfactory reports.

Your credit limit with us is $2,500. This figure will be reviewed after a year's experience, with a view to revising it upward.

We look forward to a long and pleasant business relationship. Please let us know promptly whenever you feel we can improve our service, for our aim is to be of the greatest possible service to you.

Sincerely,

John D. Lamont
Credit Manager

JDL/jk

Sample 79. Granting Credit II

ABC COMPANY, INC.
123 MAIN STREET
CENTERVILLE, IL 66666

March 15, 19XX

XX XXXXXX XX XXXXXXX
XXXXXXXXXXX
XX XXXXXXX XXX
XXXXXXXXX XX XXXXX

Dear Mr. XXXXXXX:

It is our pleasure to welcome you as a preferred customer. Your outstanding credit record places you in a very special category. Your Silver Card is being processed and will arrive in about ten days.

We have set your credit limit at $5,000. Should you at any time need a higher limit, please contact us for assistance.

We know you will find use of your Silver Card to be of great convenience and pleasure. Our staff are trained to give you that extra service that speaks louder than words ever could to tell you that we value your patronage.

Sincerely,

M. C. Robbins
Credit Manager

MCR:lk

DENYING CREDIT

There is no satisfaction in turning down a credit applicant. However, the more tactful you can be, the better the chance is that you will not have lost a customer. Your aim in writing the letter is both to convey the unpleasant news and to keep the customer's business. If you lose the customer's goodwill, you may lose more business through the customer's complaints to others.

TIPS

- Thank the person for having made the application and for showing an interest in the company.
- Make your refusal clear but as soft as possible.
- Do not belittle the applicant in any way.
- Suggest future reconsideration.

Sample 80. Denying Credit I

ABC COMPANY, INC.
123 MAIN STREET
CENTERVILLE, IL 66666

March 15, 19XX

XX XXXXXX XX XXXXXXX
XXXXXXXXXXX
XX XXXXXXX XXX
XXXXXXXXX XX XXXXX

Dear Mr. XXXXXXX:

Thank you for your application for credit.

We regret that we are unable to offer you credit at the present time. The information we have received is of a conflicting nature and has led us to this difficult decision. We will, of course, be pleased to review your application at a later time, should you request it. We are aware that temporary problems often are resolved happily.

In the meanwhile, we hope to continue to supply your needs as we have during the past several months. In order to ensure immediate handling of your order, would you kindly continue to send a check with your order, as you have been doing?

Sincerely,

M. C. Robbins
Credit Manager

MCR:lk

Sample 81. Denying Credit II

ABC COMPANY, INC.
123 MAIN STREET
CENTERVILLE, IL 66666

March 15, 19XX

XX XXXXXX XX XXXXXXX
XXXXXXXXXXX
XX XXXXXXX XXX
XXXXXXXXX XX XXXXX

Dear Mr. XXXXXXX:

Thank you for your application for an account with our company.

Unfortunately, our enquiries have led us to the reluctant decision not to extend credit to you at the present time. The problem we sense is not one of general creditworthiness, but of lateness in payment. We will be most happy to reconsider an application in time.

We look forward to being of continuing service to you and have every confidence that our products will meet your most demanding requirements.

Sincerely,

M. C. Robbins
Credit Manager

MCR:lk

INVITING AN ACCOUNT

One of the best ways of securing continuing business from a person or firm with good credit is to secure that customer as a credit account. The best way to secure that account is to ask the customer to open an account with you, to enclose a simplified application with a business reply envelope, and to indicate that the account is theirs just for the asking.

TIPS

- Start with a positive statement about the person or firm.
- Make it very plain that the reason for your writing is to offer an account.
- Mention some of the benefits that the person or firm can enjoy from the account.
- Stress how easy it is to open the account.
- Offer to answer any questions that the person or firm may have.

Sample 82. *Inviting an Account I*

ABC COMPANY, INC.
123 MAIN STREET
CENTERVILLE, IL 66666

March 15, 19XX

XX XXXXXX XX XXXXXXX
XXXXXXXXXXX
XX XXXXXXX XXX
XXXXXXXX XX XXXXX

Dear Mr. XXXXXXX:

Your splendid credit record and acknowledged business achievement makes you one of the preferred people who should be expected to carry our Silver Card.

We would be happy to issue the Silver Card upon receipt of a completed application on the Preferred Applicant form that is enclosed. Please fill in the few questions on the form, sign it, and return it to us no later than April 30, 19XX.

Not only does a Silver Card immediately make our entire range of services and products available to you, but it does so with style. Our staff has been especially trained to give preferred service to our preferred customers. A Silver Card normally includes a $5,000 credit advantage, an amount considerably more than is made available to our standard accounts.

We look forward to welcoming you as a Silver Card Preferred Customer in the very near future.

Sincerely,

M. C. Robbins
Credit Manager

MCR:lk

Sample 83. *Inviting an Account II*

ABC COMPANY, INC.
123 MAIN STREET
CENTERVILLE, IL 66666

March 15, 19XX

XX XXXXXX XX XXXXXXX
XXXXXXXXXXX
XX XXXXXXX XXX
XXXXXXXXX XX XXXXX

Dear Mr. XXXXXXX:

We are happy to welcome you to Centerville. ABC is Centerville's oldest and largest supplier of household needs. We would welcome your business and invite you to apply for an account with us.

As you go through the process of settling in, you will find constant need for quality products you can secure from us, ranging from new locks and keys to brooms and cleaners to lamps and bulbs. We carry a complete line of minor household repair items, of bathroom and linen supplies, of kitchen and cookware. Look us over and we have every confidence you'll get into the ''ABC habit'' early on in your Centerville life.

An application for an ABC account is enclosed, together with a business reply envelope. Make your shopping easier and faster by using our special ABC Accounts express line at the checkout counter. Won't you send us your application today?

Sincerely,

M. C. Robbins
Credit Manager

MCR:lk

COLLECTION LETTERS

Unfortunately, there is a need to write collection letters. In fact, collection letter writing has become quite methodical, starting with a simple reminder. If this fails, it is followed by an inquiry. This, in turn, is followed by an appeal. And the last letter is in the form of a demand. The aim of the letter is to motivate the customer to pay. In order to so motivate the customer, appeal is made to self-esteem, conscience, good reputation, and legal threat, as needed.

Fortunately, most customers are merely forgetful or lax. The reminder letter is enough to secure the bulk of late payments.

The four letters—reminder, inquiry, appeal, and demand—should be timed so as to be progressively stronger. Once payment is received, they should be stopped. Each one should contain the request to ignore this letter if payment has already been sent.

TIPS

- Always be polite. Even the demand letter should leave the door open for future business once this situation is resolved.
- Be direct. Ask for payment. Name the amount. Give a date when it is expected.
- Send your letters out in two- or three-week intervals.
- Always include a statement that invites the customer to ignore the letter if payment has already been remitted.

Sample 84. Collection Letter I (Reminder)

ABC COMPANY, INC.
123 MAIN STREET
CENTERVILLE, IL 66666

March 15, 19XX

XX XXXXXX XX XXXXXXX
XXXXXXXXXXX
XX XXXXXXX XXX
XXXXXXXXX XX XXXXX

Dear Mr. XXXXXXX:

Just a reminder that your account is past due.

Please remit $_____ today.

If you have already mailed your payment, please disregard this letter.

Many thanks,

Sincerely,

M. C. Robbins
Credit Manager

MCR:lk

Sample 85. Collection Letter II (Inquiry)

ABC COMPANY, INC.
123 MAIN STREET
CENTERVILLE, IL 66666

March 15, 19XX

XX XXXXXX XX XXXXXXX
XXXXXXXXXXX
XX XXXXXXX XXX
XXXXXXXXX XX XXXXX

Dear Mr. XXXXXXX:

Our records show that your balance of $_____ is still unpaid.

Is there some problem with this account that we are unaware of? Please let us
know if that is so, and we will be happy to work the matter out with you.

If there is no problem, would you kindly send us your payment today?

If you have already done so, please ignore this letter.

Sincerely,

M. C. Robbins
Credit Manager

MCR:lk

Sample 86. Collection Letter III (Appeal)

ABC COMPANY, INC.
123 MAIN STREET
CENTERVILLE, IL 66666

March 15, 19XX

XX XXXXXX XX XXXXXXX
XXXXXXXXXXX
XX XXXXXXX XXX
XXXXXXXXX XX XXXXX

Dear Mr. XXXXXXX:

We regret the necessity of having to call your attention to your outstanding
balance of $_____.

Won't you please mail your remittance today so you won't have to keep receiving these kinds of letters from us. They are no more pleasant for us to send than for you to receive.

Please do not disappoint us. If you have already sent us your payment, please ignore this letter.

Sincerely,

M. C. Robbins
Credit Manager

MCR:lk

Sample 87. Collection Letter IV (Demand)

ABC COMPANY, INC.
123 MAIN STREET
CENTERVILLE, IL 66666

March 15, 19XX

XX XXXXXX XX XXXXXXX
XXXXXXXXXXX
XX XXXXXXX XXX
XXXXXXXXX XX XXXXX

Dear Mr. XXXXXXX:

Since you have ignored several requests for payment of your past due account of $_____, we must now insist that you send us your check for the amount.

Unless we hear from you in five business days, we will take the unpleasant step of turning your account over to a collection agency. Neither of us wants to see your credit standing jeopardized, so we hope this step will not be necessary.

If payment has been made, please ignore this letter. If payment has not yet been made, we urge you to send your check now.

Sincerely,

M. C. Robbins
Credit Manager

MCR:lk

LETTER OF CREDIT DELINQUENCY

One form of collection letter is a letter of delinquency. Such a letter has the appearance of an official document, though it is, in fact, only the strongest—and sometimes most effective—of your series of collection letters. The more official the letter looks, the more effective it is likely to be. Some companies even have a special letterhead for these letters, such as "Office of the Attorney" or "Collection Services." If the letterhead conveys the sense that it comes from outside your company, it is even more effective.

TIPS

- Do not be personal. Give the letter an official appearance.
- Include the customer's name, address, account number, amount due, and the name of your collection agency. Merely the mention of the name of your collection agency is usually enough to secure payment.

Sample 88. **Letter of Credit Delinquency**

OFFICE OF THE ATTORNEY
ABC COMPANY, INC.
123 MAIN STREET
CENTERVILLE, IL 66666

NOTICE OF DELINQUENCY

March 15, 19XX

You owe $_____, which is past due since _____.

        Mr. XXXXXX XX XXXXXXX
        XXXXXXXXXXX
        XX XXXXXXX XXX
        XXXXXXXXX XX XXXXX

We are required to turn over your account to the XXXXXX XXXXXXX Collection Agency.

Such a step will, of course, place your credit standing in serious jeopardy. To avoid this action, you must settle your account with us in full and at once.

APOLOGY FOR A COLLECTION LETTER SENT IN ERROR

Occasionally, you will send a collection letter in error to a customer in good standing. When this happens, send a letter of apology.

TIPS

- Acknowledge that a mistake has been made and simply apologize.
- Include your regret for any inconvenience or embarrassment.
- Assure the customer that you will do all you can to avoid repeating the mistake.
- Ask for continued patronage.

Sample 89. Apology for a Collection Letter Sent in Error I

ABC COMPANY, INC.
123 MAIN STREET
CENTERVILLE, IL 66666

March 15, 19XX

XX XXXXXX XX XXXXXXX
XXXXXXXXXXX
XX XXXXXXX XXX
XXXXXXXXX XX XXXXX

Dear Mr. XXXXXXX:

The collection letter you recently received from us was sent in error. We are red-faced, to say the least.

We apologize for our clerical error, assure you that your account with us is in very good order, and will do all in our power to make sure that such an error does not happen again.

We look forward to continuing to serve you.

Sincerely,

M. C. Robbins
Credit Manager

MCR:lk

Sample 90. Apology for a Collection Letter Sent in Error II

ABC COMPANY, INC.
123 MAIN STREET
CENTERVILLE, IL 66666

March 15, 19XX

XX XXXXXX XX XXXXXX
XXXXXXXXXX
XX XXXXXX XXX
XXXXXXXXX XX XXXXX

Dear Mr. XXXXXXX:

Your account with us is in good order! We erroneously sent you a collection
letter—and now send you our sincere apologies.

These mistakes don't happen very often. We're sorry it happened with such a good
customer as you. Be assured we'll try to make certain there's no repeat. We hope
that our mistake did not cause you any embarrassment or inconvenience.

We anticipate being of continued service to you in the days ahead.

Sincerely,

M. C. Robbins
Credit Manager

MCR:lk

COLLECTION LETTER TO AN OLD CUSTOMER

Sometimes an old and valued customer delays payment. Your letter should acknowledge
the length and strength of your long-lasting business relationship. In a letter to such a customer
asking for payment, you want to stress your desire for a continuation of your relationship.

TIPS

- Refer to your pleasure in the relationship you have had over the years with the customer
  and give assurance that you understand things can be difficult once in a while.
- Provide some way for the person or firm to save face.
- If this is a single incidence, offer to be of some help in handling payments in order to
  maintain the business relationship.
- Tell the customer that you are fully confident that payment will be made.

Sample 91. Collection Letter to an Old Customer I

ABC COMPANY, INC.
123 MAIN STREET
CENTERVILLE, IL 66666

March 15, 19XX

XX XXXXXX XX XXXXXX
XXXXXXXXXXX
XX XXXXXXX XXX
XXXXXXXXX XX XXXXX

Dear Mr. XXXXXXX:

Our business relationship over the years has been a matter of great pleasure and satisfaction to us. You will understand that my reason for writing is aimed to foster and deepen that relationship.

Your account with us is in arrears to an extent that causes some concern in our accounting department. We recognize the seasonable nature of your business and the problems with cash flow that result from this. As you know, we have always been willing to work out mutually satisfactory arrangements during this time of the year.

Would you kindly give me a ring at the end of next week so we can determine together how best the account is to be handled in the immediate future.

I have every confidence that you will understand that this letter is written with the motive of enhancing our continuing relationship as well as getting through this present situation.

Sincerely,

M. C. Robbins
Credit Manager

MCR:lk

Sample 92. Collection Letter to an Old Customer II

ABC COMPANY, INC.
123 MAIN STREET
CENTERVILLE, IL 66666

March 15, 19XX

XX XXXXXX XX XXXXXXX
XXXXXXXXXXX
XX XXXXXXX XXX
XXXXXXXXX XX XXXXX

Dear Mr. XXXXXXX:

We at ABC value your long—term business relationship with us.

A review of your account shows that some time has passed since you last made payment to us. If there is some difficulty you are facing that is causing this, we would like the opportunity of working matters out with you. If this is the result of an oversight, we would appreciate early remittance.

We look forward to hearing from you in the near future.

Sincerely,

M. C. Robbins
Credit Manager

MCR:lk

CHAPTER 8

Letters for Special Occasions

In every business there are special times and occasions when a letter helps the business, expresses an opinion, or answers a need. This chapter contains samples of such letters. They are not part of everyday business life, but they do fill a need when the occasion arises.

ACCEPTING AN INVITATION

You may be invited to address a meeting, accept an office, represent your company, or receive an award. In your letter of acceptance, you should repeat what it is you are accepting so any possible misunderstandings about the nature of the invitation can be cleared up at once.

TIPS

- State your pleasure at being invited. Indicate that you are pleased to accept the invitation.
- Make it clear what you are accepting. If it involves a time, date, and place, repeat them as confirmation.

Sample 93. Accepting an Invitation I

ABC COMPANY, INC.
123 MAIN STREET
CENTERVILLE, IL 66666

March 15, 19XX

XXX XXXXXX XX XXXXXXXXXX
XXXXXXXXXXX
XX XXXXXXX XXX
XXXXXXXXX XX XXXXX

Dear Mr. XXXXXXXXXX:

Thank you so very much for your kind invitation to address the Centerville Booster Club monthly luncheon at 12 p.m., April 23, at the Hotel Commodore Admiralty Room on the subject of "The Place of Expert Systems in Business During the Next Decade." I am pleased to accept your invitation.

This is a topic that is uppermost in the minds of many businesses these days as a matter of urgent business survival. Yet it is also a topic about which there is much misunderstanding. I hope to generate more light than heat in my remarks. I plan to take about twenty minutes for the main part of my address and would like to have questions from the floor for the rest of the time allotted to me.

I look forward to this opportunity of being with you and the Booster Club members once again.

Sincerely,

John P. Rogers
President

amc

Sample 94. Accepting an Invitation II

ABC COMPANY, INC.
123 MAIN STREET
CENTERVILLE, IL 66666

March 15, 19XX

XXX XXXXXX XX XXXXXXXXXX
XXXXXXXXXXX
XX XXXXXXX XXX
XXXXXXXXX XX XXXXX

Dear Mr. XXXXXXXXXX:

Thank you for asking me to accept the "Man of the Year" Award for the Expert Systems Association of Illinois. I accept the honor with much pleasure, although I can think of many in our field who are more deserving. Surely their turn will come in the years ahead.

In your invitation you asked me to accept the award in person at the annual meeting of the association on May 3, to be held at the Fairmont Country Club in Midvale at 7:30 p.m. I have made adjustments in my schedule to be able to attend, together with Mrs. Rogers. For us this is a black-tie occasion in spirit as well as in dress.

Please express my appreciation to the members of the selection committee.

Mrs. Rogers and I look forward to the occasion with much anticipation.

Sincerely,

John P. Rogers
President

amc

DECLINING AN INVITATION

Sometimes it is necessary or desirable to decline an invitation to speak to a meeting, accept an award, or accept an office. Decline with regret. Give a short reason for declining, without going into complex background.

TIPS

- Mention the nature of the invitation that you are declining.
- Express your appreciation for being asked.
- Give a short, uncomplicated reason for declining.
- Make yourself available for reconsideration at a later date if you wish to do so.

Sample 95. Declining an Invitation I

ABC COMPANY, INC.
123 MAIN STREET
CENTERVILLE, IL 66666

March 15, 19XX

XXX XXXXXX XX XXXXXXXXXX
XXXXXXXXXXX
XX XXXXXXX XXX
XXXXXXXXX XX XXXXX

Dear Mr. XXXXXXXXXX:

Thank you for your kind invitation to address the Centerville Booster Club on May 23 on the topic of "The Place of Expert Systems in Business During the Next Decade."

I regret that I am not able to accept your invitation at this time. My schedule calls for me to be in Asia on a consultative assignment with the Department of the Air Force during the entire month of May.

I very much enjoy being with you and Booster Club members. Should you invite me to speak at a future meeting, I will do my best to see that my calendar is clear.

Thanks so much for thinking of me.

Sincerely,

John P. Rogers
President

amc

Sample 96. Declining an Invitation II

ABC COMPANY, INC.
123 MAIN STREET
CENTERVILLE, IL 66666

March 15, 19XX

XXX XXXXXX XX XXXXXXXXX
XXXXXXXXXX
XX XXXXXXX XXX
XXXXXXXXX XX XXXXX

Dear Mr. XXXXXXXXXX:

Thank you for offering me the position of chairman of the 19XX Community United Services Drive.

It is with considerable regret that I must decline your kind invitation. My business schedule during 19XX is such that I would not be able to give the drive the attention it deserves.

Please express my deep appreciation to the nominating committee for their confidence.

I wish you and your colleagues well in your continued endeavors for the betterment of our community.

Sincerely,

John P. Rogers
President

amc

LETTER OF COMPLIMENT

Every speaker or community leader appreciates knowing that his speech or efforts are recognized and valued. A short letter that compliments the person is a good way of doing a nice thing and of winning a friend.

TIPS

- Be specific. Name the time and place, the name of the organization, the title or subject of the speech.
- Point out some personal benefit you have derived from the person's presentation or service.
- Express good wishes for the future.

Sample 97. Letter of Compliment I

ABC COMPANY, INC.
123 MAIN STREET
CENTERVILLE, IL 66666

March 15, 19XX

XXX XXXXXX XX XXXXXXXXX
XXXXXXXXXXX
XX XXXXXXX XXX
XXXXXXXXX XX XXXXX

Dear Mr. XXXXXXXXXX:

Your address to the annual meeting of the Expert Systems Association of Illinois on the topic of "How to Use Expert Systems as a Business Weapon" was outstanding. I have not heard such a succinct and dramatic summary of this vital topic.

Several members of the association have telephoned me to express their appreciation of the address and of your dynamic presentation.

We all look forward to reading your article on the subject in the next issue of the national association journal.

With much appreciation, I remain

Yours sincerely,

John P. Rogers
Chairman, Program Committee
Expert Systems Association of Illinois

amc

Sample 98. Letter of Compliment II

ABC COMPANY, INC.
123 MAIN STREET
CENTERVILLE, IL 66666

March 15, 19XX

XXX XXXXXX XX XXXXXXXXX
XXXXXXXXXX
XX XXXXXXX XXX
XXXXXXXX XX XXXXX

Dear Mr. XXXXXXXXXX:

As you conclude your term as chairman of the 19XX Community United Services
Drive, I want you to know how much your leadership has been appreciated.

You have given the drive a focus that has enabled the participating businesses
to know what is expected of them, to understand what is happening to their
contributions, and to have the right information to make the best possible
presentation to their employees. We have never had such a helpful kit to aid us
in making our community's needs known to our people.

The success of the drive this year is testimony to the dynamic of your
leadership. Our thanks to you for making our part easier and more effective than
ever before.

Well done from all of us at ABC!

Sincerely,

John P. Rogers
President

amc

REQUESTING PERMISSION TO USE COPYRIGHTED MATERIAL

In the preparation of reports, articles, or manuscripts, it is sometimes useful to include
material that has been published elsewhere. Unless this material is in the public domain (generally, material that was published more than fifty-four years ago and that has not been re-
vised—Abraham Lincoln's Gettysburg Address is an example of published material that is in
the public domain), it is copyrighted. Some person or some company owns the rights to that
material. It is both courteous and a matter of legal prudence to request permission to reprint
the material. Previously published copyrighted material can include text, illustrations, charts,
table, photographs, and the like.

If you plan to use the copyrighted material within your company or for a nonprofit purpose, permission is normally given without charge. If, however, you plan to use the material in a profit-making venture, a fee may well be asked. The amount of the fee depends on the amount of material you wish to use as well as the nature of the final product you are preparing.

Sometimes the company that originally published the material has gone out of business or has been merged with another firm. You may not be able to locate the present holder of the copyright, especially if those rights have been transferred several times. A copy of your letter to the last known rights holder in which you ask for permission should be kept on file, however. This will show that you tried to secure permission from the last known rights holder in case the present rights holder reads your product and raises questions about the use of the material.

TIPS

- Send the letter in duplicate with a place for the permission to be granted. The rights holder can keep one copy and return the second to you.
- Tell the rights holder exactly what material you want to use, in what kind of product you want to use it, how many copies of the product will be published, and whether it will be sold for a profit. If so, how much will the product be sold for.
- Express your thanks for giving permission.

Sample 99. Requesting Permission to Use Copyrighted Material I

ABC COMPANY, INC.
123 MAIN STREET
CENTERVILLE, IL 66666

March 15, 19XX

XXX XXXXXX XX XXXXXXXXXX
XXXXXXXXXXX
XX XXXXXXX XXX
XXXXXXXXX XX XXXXX

Dear Mr. XXXXXXXXXX:

I am preparing a report for circulation to stockholders and officers of our company on projected trends in the microcomputer market and our projected place in the market. We will distribute without charge a total of about 350 copies.

You prepared a fine graph analysis of projected microcomputer sales for the next decade. This analysis was recently printed in <u>Microcomputer</u> <u>Forecasts</u>, a newsletter published by the Info Corporation.

We would very much appreciate your permission to reproduce this graph in our report. Unless you indicate otherwise, we would provide the following credit line:

Reprinted with the kind permission of XXXXXXXXX.

Please initial the two copies of this letter in the appropriate place and return one copy to us. The other copy is for your records. A business reply envelope is enclosed for your convenience. We will be pleased to send you a copy of the report.

Thank you for your help in this matter.

Sincerely,

John P. Rogers
President

amc

Date:_____

Check one: Permission granted_____   Permission denied_____

By:_____ , XXXXXXXXXXX (Company name)

Sample 100. Requesting Permission to Use Copyrighted Material II

ABC COMPANY, INC.
123 MAIN STREET
CENTERVILLE, IL 66666

March 15, 19XX

XXX XXXXXX XX XXXXXXXXXX
XXXXXXXXXXX
XX XXXXXXX XXX
XXXXXXXXX XX XXXXX

Dear Mr. XXXXXXXXX:

We are writing a technical article for publication in the Journal of Microcomputer Studies. This journal is a professional publication for researchers and management in the field of microcomputer technical development. The journal has a paid circulation of 1,500 copies quarterly and is published by the not-for-profit Society for the Advancement of Microcomputer Research.

In the article we are preparing, entitled "Microchip Modifications for LISP Language Processing," we would like to quote from your book The History of LISP.

The actual three—sentence quotation we would like to use is found on page 267 and is attached.

Unless you indicate otherwise, we would use the following credit line as a footnote:

© 19XX by XXXXXXXXXXX. Used with permission.

Please sign the release statement below and return a copy to us in the self—addressed, stamped envelope. We will, of course, send you a complimentary copy of the journal issue in which the article appears.

Thank you for your generous cooperation.

Sincerely,

John P. Rogers
President

amc

Date:_____

Check one: Permission granted_____ Permission denied_____

Signed: _____

LETTER OF PRAISE TO AN OUTSIDE FIRM

There are times when the services you receive from an outside firm are so excellent that you want to send a special letter of thanks to the management of the firm. This kind of letter creates a deep reservoir of good feelings, which will probably make future relations even better.

TIPS

- Make your thanks genuine, without overstatement.
- Make it clear what prompted you to write this letter.
- If possible, single out a particularly helpful person.

Sample 101. Letter of Praise to an Outside Firm I

ABC COMPANY, INC.
123 MAIN STREET
CENTERVILLE, IL 66666

March 15, 19XX

XXX XXXXXX XX XXXXXXXXXX
XXXXXXXXXXX
XX XXXXXXX XXX
XXXXXXXXX XX XXXXX

Dear Mr. XXXXXXXXXX:

For the past four years we at ABC have been using your travel agency to make our business travel arrangements.

We have always been very pleased with the thoroughness and personal attention your staff has given to our requirements. However, we recently placed an extraordinary demand on your staff for services related to a regional industry convention which we sponsored in Centerville. Your staff, and especially Ms Mansard, outdid themselves in courtesy, efficiency, and service—and under pressure circumstances.

Please convey to your entire crew our gratitude and respect.

Sincerely,

John P. Rogers
President

amc

Sample 102. *Letter of Praise to an Outside Firm II*

ABC COMPANY, INC.
123 MAIN STREET
CENTERVILLE, IL 66666

March 15, 19XX

XXX   XXXXXX XX XXXXXXXXXX
XXXXXXXXXXX
XX XXXXXXX XXX
XXXXXXXXX XX XXXXX

Dear Mr. XXXXXXXXXX:

Last Tuesday we held a twenty-fifth-anniversary dinner to honor one of our staff. The dinner was held in the Regency Room.

In all my years of attending such functions, I have seldom seen such excellent handling of all details. From the car valet who knew about the occasion and where it was to be, all the way to the checkroom girl who kept all our coats separate for easy handling when we were finished, every possibility was anticipated and prepared for.

Please express our thanks especially to the chef and his assistants who made the meal so enjoyable and to the waiters in the Regency Room who served with such "elegant invisibleness."

We certainly look forward to holding another such occasion there.

Sincerely,

John P. Rogers
President

amc

LETTER TO A PUBLIC OFFICIAL

There are times you wish to express an opinion or concern to an elected or appointed public official. Such a letter is quite in keeping with running your business, since public officials need to know what their constituents think about matters that have to be voted on or decided. It is even appropriate to write a letter on an issue that does not directly relate to your business. Public officials are sensitive to the concerns of community and business leaders.

TIPS

- Keep the letter to one page.
- As much as possible, keep your letter positive—with more reason than emotion.
- State your concern briefly in the opening paragraph.
- Be sure your recommendations are brief and clearly expressed.

Sample 103. Letter to a Public Official I

ABC COMPANY, INC.
123 MAIN STREET
CENTERVILLE, IL 66666

March 15, 19XX

The Hon. XXXXXX XX XXXXXXXXXX
House of Representatives
Washington, DC 20510

Dear Congressman XXXXXXXXX:

You are a member of the committee that is holding hearings next week on the pirating of proprietary computer software programs. As a leader in the field of software program development, we have a crucial interest in this topic. Our firm—and the scores of individual free-lance software programmers who provide services to us under royalty contracts—lose millions of dollars in revenue annually because companies and individuals illegally copy our software products.

Present copyright laws were not written to apply to computer software. We need strengthened legislation to make software piracy a felonious act rather than merely a civil misdemeanor. By so strengthening the law—and hence our ability to pursue flagrant violators in court under significant possible penalty—we believe that the level of piracy will greatly diminish.

Strengthened laws against software piracy would, of course, enhance government revenue income at both the local and federal level, since taxes would be paid on legally purchased software. The value of lost sales due to the present lax laws amounts to more than $5 billion annually!

We have every confidence you will exert your influence on behalf of strengthened protection for computer software developers at the committee hearings next week. We would be pleased to provide your staff with any background that would be useful in preparing for the hearings.

Sincerely,

John P. Rogers
President

amc

Sample 104. *Letter to a Public Official II*

ABC COMPANY, INC.
123 MAIN STREET
CENTERVILLE, IL 66666

March 15, 19XX

The Hon. XXXXXX XX XXXXXXXXXX
City Hall
Centerville, IL 66666

Dear Mayor XXXXXXXXXX:

We recognize that in many decisions there is no clear "right" or "wrong" decision. A "trade-off" decision has to be made between many desirable and undesirable results that flow from each of the decision options.

We must nevertheless lodge our strongest protest against the decision you made last week to suspend operation of the Centerville Visitor and Convention Center. In order to save a few thousand dollars of budgeted operating costs, you are going to lose millions of dollars of business for Centerville merchants, hotels, and restaurants annually. Your decision was made on too limited a basis. It should be reversed immediately.

As one of Centerville's businesses that acts as host to literally hundreds of individual business visitors each year, we know how extensively our guests use the services of the Visitor and Convention Center. We also know from experience how helpful the center has been in assisting us to bring scores of industry meetings to Centerville over the past five years. If Centerville loses the services of the center, we predict an early drop in the number of business conventions in our city.

We are pleased to support you in most of your decisions and are grateful for the vigorous leadership you give Centerville. Here is a chance for you to show unusual courage and sound second—thinking by reversing your decision to close the center. We urge you to do so without delay.

Sincerely,

John P. Rogers
President

amc

CHAPTER 9

Letters for Better Community Relations

Businesses operate in a number of environments. One is the internal environment of the company itself: what the business does, who does it, how it is done. Another is the legal environment: the web of local, state, and federal laws and regulations that impinge on a business's activities. Another is the industry or trade environment: the place of the business in relation to other businesses in the same or related industries or trade. And there is the community environment: the people and neighborhood in which the business is located.

Many businesses encourage participation in community activities and organizations. This involvement may be undertaken as part of one's business responsibility or as a personal choice. Letters that are written in fulfilling these community responsibilities influence community attitudes about your company as well as yourself.

As soon as you begin to get involved, you will inevitably be asked to become increasingly more active. Every community organization, committee, or board is always looking for responsible people who will participate. By participating in one activity, you come to the attention of leaders in other activities. This begins the onrush of invitations. You should take special care over the wording of your letters that turn down an invitation. You want to be clear in your refusal; you do not want to raise undue expectations about your future availability; you want your refusal to result in positive feelings about you and your company even though you said no.

ACCEPTING AN INVITATION

You may be invited to become a member of a committee, board, commission, or organization in the community and wish to accept the invitation. Your letter of acceptance can be brief; it will certainly be welcome.

TIPS

- Say how pleased you are to accept the invitation.
- Indicate that you consider it an honor to be asked to serve.
- Offer information about any area of special knowledge or experience that you have, if appropriate.
- If your period of service will be limited to a certain period of time, state this in your letter of acceptance. It will make it easier to avoid possible misunderstanding when you later resign, since the terms of your service were clear to all from the beginning.

Sample 105. Accepting an Invitation I

ABC COMPANY, INC.
123 MAIN STREET
CENTERVILLE, IL 66666

March 15, 19XX

XXX   XXXXXX XX XXXXXXXXXX
XXXXXXXXXXX
XX XXXXXXX XXX
XXXXXXXXX XX XXXXX

Dear Mr. XXXXXXXXXX:

Thank you for your invitation to serve as a member of the City Solid Waste Commission. I'm pleased to accept and deem it an honor to be counted among those whose judgment and experience is sought on this vital health and environmental issue.

Because of the press of commitments already made, I'll be able to sit on the commission only until September 19XX. During that period I hope, with the help of the other members of the commission, to come to grips with the primary issues facing us in finding a suitable alternative to our present method of disposing of solid waste. I shall be happy to make available to the commission without cost our computer facilities to run projection scenarios on the various options we will consider.

I plan to attend the next meeting of the commission on April 4 at 7:30 p.m. in Room 243 in City Hall.

Sincerely,

John P. Rogers
President

amc

Sample 106. Accepting an Invitation II

ABC COMPANY, INC.
123 MAIN STREET
CENTERVILLE, IL 66666

March 15, 19XX

XXX   XXXXXX XX XXXXXXXXXX
XXXXXXXXXXX
XX XXXXXXXX XXX
XXXXXXXXXX XX XXXXX

Dear Mr. XXXXXXXXXX:

I'm pleased to accept membership on the board of the Centerville Chapter of the
Cerebral Palsy Foundation.

I have always admired the staff and volunteers of the foundation, who have so
unstintingly given themselves to serve the physical, emotional, and practical
needs of those stricken with cerebral palsy. It is an honor to be asked to assist
in enabling them to do their work with greater community support.

One of the contributions I hope to be able to make is to form a President's
Circle of Centerville business and industry leaders, who will take the cause of
the foundation to heart and marshal increased popular and financial support for
the cause.

Please extend to the members of the board my appreciation for their invitation.
I plan to attend the April 27 meeting.

Sincerely,

John P. Rogers
President

amc

CONTRIBUTION TO A CHARITABLE CAUSE

When your business makes a contribution to a charitable cause, a covering letter should accompany your check. This letter, together with others of past years in the file, serves as a ready reference to your continuing relationship with the charity. The file will aid you in determining the extent of your support for the cause.

TIPS

- Say how pleased you are to support such a worthy cause.
- Be brief; mention the amount contributed; wish the charity well in its endeavors.
- If this is not a company contribution but you are using a company letterhead, be sure to mention that this is a personal contribution.

Sample 107. Contribution to a Charitable Cause I

ABC COMPANY, INC.
123 MAIN STREET
CENTERVILLE, IL 66666

March 15, 19XX

XXX XXXXXX XX XXXXXXXXXX
XXXXXXXXXXX
XX XXXXXXX XXX
XXXXXXXXX XX XXXXX

Dear Mr. XXXXXXXXXX:

It is with great satisfaction that I enclose our company check for $_____ as our 19XX contribution to the United Campaign of Centerville.

We value the services rendered to our community by the numerous charities that are part of the United Campaign. We are pleased to have this opportunity to help make possible the continuance of these services during these difficult days.

With all good wishes, I remain

Yours sincerely,

John P. Rogers
President

amc

Sample 108. Contribution to a Charitable Cause II

ABC COMPANY, INC.
123 MAIN STREET
CENTERVILLE, IL 66666

March 15, 19XX

XXX XXXXXX XX XXXXXXXXXX
XXXXXXXXXXX
XX XXXXXX XXX
XXXXXXXXX XX XXXXX

Dear Mr. XXXXXXXXXX:

The Kidney Fund has meant a great deal to me personally ever since my father had a kidney transplant and lived for another ten years. The surgeon explained that much of the research that lay behind the development of this surgical technique was funded by the Kidney Fund.

I am happy to contribute $_____ for now. Please note in your records that this is a personal, rather than a company, contribution.

My family and I wish you well in your continued research and donor—matching efforts.

Sincerely,

John P. Rogers
President

amc

REFUSING TO CONTRIBUTE TO A CHARITABLE CAUSE

Every business receives many more requests to support worthy causes than it has the resources to underwrite. Accordingly, you will have to refuse to contribute to a number of requests each year. One way to do so is simply to ignore the request. In fact, fund-raising programs are based on certain standard percentages of response, recognizing that the bulk of appeals will be ignored.

However, if the charity is a local one and the leadership of the charity is made up of people in the community whose goodwill you value, a tactful letter refusing to contribute will not cost you the goodwill that ignoring the appeal might.

TIPS

- Acknowledge the value of the cause you have been asked to support.
- Do not go into a long discussion of reasons why you are not sending a contribution.
- If you really mean it, raise the possibility of a contribution at a later time.

Sample 109. Refusing to Contribute to a Charitable Cause I

ABC COMPANY, INC.
123 MAIN STREET
CENTERVILLE, IL 66666

March 15, 19XX

XXX XXXXX XX XXXXXXXXXX
XXXXXXXXXXX
XX XXXXXX XXX
XXXXXXXXX XX XXXXX

Dear Mr. XXXXXXXXXX:

We appreciate the opportunity you, the Centerville Chapter of International Student Exchange, have given us to contribute to the support of a foreign high school student at Centerville High next year.

We have concluded with regret that we are unable to make such a contribution this year. We are fully behind the fine work you are doing, confident that a more peaceful world through international understanding at the family level is but one of the benefits from your exchange program. Unfortunately, our budget for the year is closed and all allocations for contributions have been made.

May I suggest you send us a request prior to September 1, 19XX, for next year's exchange program. We will then consider it during our budget-making period, along with other community requests.

We wish you well in your efforts this year and trust it will be possible for us to participate more directly next year.

Sincerely,

John P. Rogers
President

amc

Sample 110. Refusing to Contribute to a Charitable Cause II

ABC COMPANY, INC.
123 MAIN STREET
CENTERVILLE, IL 66666

March 15, 19XX

XXX XXXXXX XX XXXXXXXXX
XXXXXXXXXXX
XX XXXXXX XXX
XXXXXXXX XX XXXXX

Dear Mr. XXXXXXXXXX:

I'm sorry to tell you that ABC cannot send you a contribution for 19XX.

Our industry has experienced a difficult time this year, and unfortunately, we have been affected. We are severely curtailing certain expenses, including the ratio of our contributions budget.

Our decision not to send a contribution this year in no way indicates less enthusiasm for the good work you are doing. We hope this will be only a temporary situation and that next year we will be able to make a significant contribution to your fine program.

We do hope that you will top your goal for this year.

Sincerely,

John P. Rogers
President

amc

REQUEST FOR ZONING MODIFICATION

Businesses are located in areas of a community that have been zoned for business use. As zoning regulations change or as business needs change, you may have occasion to write the appropriate board about zoning matters. You may write to try to influence an impending zoning regulation. Or you may write to request a variance for your own business.

Your letter to the zoning body becomes a matter of public record. It should therefore deal objectively with the issue. An expression of anger will not help your cause.

TIPS

• Do your homework. Be accurate in your citation of zoning regulations and property descriptions.

- Be brief and to the point. Say clearly what you want or what your opinion is.
- Show how there will be no detriment to the community if your request for a variance is granted.
- Offer to provide any additional information needed for a fair decision.
- Be polite and respectful, but don't plead.

Sample 111. Request for Zoning Modification I

ABC COMPANY, INC.
123 MAIN STREET
CENTERVILLE, IL 66666

March 15, 19XX

XXX XXXXXX XX XXXXXXXXXX
XXXXXXXXXXX
XX XXXXXXX XXX
XXXXXXXXX XX XXXXX

Dear Mr. XXXXXXXXXX:

We own Lot 407 on Page 24 of the 19XX Tax Map of Centerville. The street address is 10 Beech Drive.

At present, the lot is divided about equally between Residential District and Limited Business District (see enclosed lot plan). This zoning condition for the lot has been in effect since zoning was first applied to this part of the city. Zoning Bylaw 101.4 states that "if a lot is divided into two zoning districts at the time of original zoning, an owner may seek a variance to have the entire lot zoned for either of the two zones, which variance shall not unreasonably be withheld by the zoning board."

We request that the entire lot at 10 Beech Drive be zoned as Limited Business. As you can see from the lot plan, the present Residential portion of the lot abuts marshland, on which houses cannot by law be built. There will therefore be no detrimental effect on any present or future residential neighborhood if this request is granted.

If you wish further documentation to consider this request, please let me know.

Thank you for your early attention to this matter.

Sincerely,

John P. Rogers
President

amc

Encl: Lot plan for 10 Beech Drive, Centerville

Sample 112. Request for Zoning Modification II

ABC COMPANY, INC.
123 MAIN STREET
CENTERVILLE, IL 66666

March 15, 19XX

XXX XXXXXX XX XXXXXXXXXX
XXXXXXXXXXX
XX XXXXXXX XXX
XXXXXXXX XX XXXXX

Dear Mr. XXXXXXXXXX:

We understand that the Zoning Board is considering changing the zoning of Main Street east of State Street to Limited Business instead of the present General Business classification.

Although our own business would not be directly jeopardized by such a zoning change because of "preexistent use" (the "grandfather" clause), we still wish to lodge a strong protest against this zoning change. We have been urging companies located elsewhere who supply us with goods and services to relocate near us or to set up a branch location close to ours. At least three of these companies have voiced officially their intent to do so. These new businesses would provide approximately 210 new jobs for Centerville, plus a significant tax base increase.

If the zoning change is passed, these businesses would not be able to locate close to us. There is every probability they would remain where they are. The loss to Centerville would be considerable, both in real tax income and in actual jobs.

I shall be pleased to provide you with all the data you desire concerning this situation and will, of course, attend the public hearing on the zoning change. In the meantime, we respectfully request that you table indefinitely consideration of this zoning change.

Sincerely,

John P. Rogers
President

amc

INVITATION TO A RECEPTION

There are occasions in the life of a business for which you hold a reception or open house for special customers, community leaders, or business colleagues. You may honor newly appointed officers, celebrate an anniversary of the business, introduce distinguished visitors, or have an exhibition. A letter of invitation or a printed invitation card to such a reception or open house provides the opportunity of bringing your business to the attention of others, even though they are unable to attend. Everyone likes to be considered important enough to be invited, so you create a reservoir of goodwill with every invitation.

TIPS

- Unless it is a black-tie occasion, make the invitation informal in tone. You want to give people the feeling that they can drop in from their daily life rather than have to dress especially for the occasion.
- Convey in your tone and description of the event that the occasion is well worth the time and effort it takes to attend. Unless you are enthusiastic, the invitation will sound dull.
- Be very clear about time, date, and place.
- If special parking arrangements have been made, describe them clearly.

Sample 113. Invitation to a Reception I

ABC COMPANY, INC.
123 MAIN STREET
CENTERVILLE, IL 66666

March 15, 19XX

XXX XXXXXX XX XXXXXXXXXX
XXXXXXXXXXX
XX XXXXXXX XXX
XXXXXXXXX XX XXXXX

Dear Mr. XXXXXXXXXX:

We hope you can join us for our Fifth Birthday Party. On April 20 we are celebrating our fifth anniversary of being in business in Centerville and our move to the new location on Main Street.

We are having an Open House from 2:30 to 5:30 p.m. on April 20 at 123 Main Street. There will be continuous informal tours of our new premises. Refreshments will be served. Our entire staff will be on hand to welcome you and answer any questions you may have.

Do drop in—if only for a few minutes—and participate with us in this happy occasion.

We are glad to count you as a friend and hope to see you then.

Very sincerely,

John P. Rogers
President

amc

Sample 114. Invitation to a Reception II (Formal printed card)

The Board of Directors and Officers
of ABC Company, Inc.
cordially invite you to
the First Annual Computer Graphics Exhibit
of students of the Centerville Middle School

Noon to 7:30 P.M.   April 22, 19XX

123 Main Street, Centerville, Illinois

Refreshments served

CHAPTER 10

Letters to Employees

Employees appreciate positive, informative letters from the boss, whether from the president of the company or from the immediate supervisor. The "occasional" letter—a letter written upon an occasion—to an employee helps foster good morale. Such letters provide employees with a sense of being on the inside, of having personal information about the company and its plans, of being more than just one of the crowd. A letter has much more of a personal touch than does a memo, and very much more than a formal, posted announcement.

Certainly the "occasional" letter should be written on the occasion of a promotion and major anniversary. Letters might also be written on occasions of increased benefits, new company directions, changes in company organization, the introduction of new product lines, and the like. Where the letter is to be sent to a large number of recipients, word-processing list and merge capabilities make the task possible with relatively little secretarial effort.

An "occasional" letter to an employee is best sent to the employee's home, rather than distributed in interoffice mail. Sending the letter to the home is a subtle way of saying, "You are more than an employee to us; you are also a person whom we care about and who has another life outside the company." The employee is flattered by this thoughtfulness.

WELCOME TO A NEW EMPLOYEE

An employee's first days with a company are filled with a blend of excitement, anxiety, strangeness, fear, challenge, satisfaction, and hope. Your letter of welcome can help allay some of the fears and uncertainties, assuring the person of a warm and enthusiastic welcome.

Your letter of welcome can also serve as a confirmation of title, starting date, responsibility, and even salary if you wish. The naming of these matters avoids any possibility of misunderstanding at the start.

TIPS

- Make your letter warm, enthusiastic, and positive.
- If you give salary and responsibility information, be complete and specific.
- Provide some challenge for the new employee to meet during the first few weeks on the job.
- Express your pleasure that the new employee is now a part of the company team.

Sample 115. Welcome to a New Employee I

ABC COMPANY, INC.
123 MAIN STREET
CENTERVILLE, IL 66666

March 15, 19XX

XXX XXXXXX XX XXXXXXXXXX
XXXXXXXXXXX
XX XXXXXXX XXX
XXXXXXXXX XX XXXXX

Dear Mr. XXXXXXXXXX:

I take great pleasure in welcoming you to the ABC Company. We look forward to seeing you on April 15 for your first day in the office.

The position of assistant national sales manager is an important one in our structure. Not only are you an understudy and assistant to the national sales manager, but you are our chief headquarters scout to sense what our competition is planning to produce two years from now. The reason we have placed this vital task as a sales-related assignment is that our sales force is in an excellent position to serve as the "eyes and ears" of the company. They are often the first to pick up industry rumors—many of which turn out to be based on real developments. Your close working relationship with our sales force on a day-to-day basis places you in a key position for hearing things first and for evaluating possible industry trends. You have our "Employee Benefits" brochure. If you have any questions about how any of these benefits apply to you, please let me or Tom McKindrey know.

Again, welcome to the team. We work hard at ABC, and we enjoy the challenge of delivering more value to our customers in this fast-changing business. We have every confidence that you will enjoy taking up this challenge with us.

Sincerely,

John P. Rogers
President

amc

Sample 116. Welcome to a New Employee II

ABC COMPANY, INC.
123 MAIN STREET
CENTERVILLE, IL 66666

March 15, 19XX

XXX XXXXXX XX XXXXXXXXXX
XXXXXXXXXXX
XX XXXXXXX XXX
XXXXXXXXX XX XXXXX

Dear Mr. XXXXXXXXXX:

On April 15, 19XX, at 9 a.m., your career with the ABC Company will begin. We have every confidence that you are looking forward to this with as much expectation as we are. We admired your work at the XYZ Corporation for many years. It is a matter of deep personal satisfaction to me that you saw a greater challenge to your talents with us as our senior research fellow.

As we have discussed together, we want to give you the maximum resources within our own structure and budget to undertake developmental research in natural language programming. And as we have discussed, there are certain nondisclosure statements that must be signed to protect our investment in these valuable developments. These statements are enclosed for your perusal and signature. Please return them to me prior to April 15.

When you come in on the fifteenth, please come directly to my office. I want to take you around and introduce you to the key people with whom you will be working regularly.

With expectations for long and fruitful years together, I am

Yours sincerely,

John P. Rogers
President

amc

CONGRATULATIONS ON A PROMOTION

Promotions are always happy times. Even if the salary increase was not as large as the employee hoped for, there is great joy over the fact of the promotion and what it portends for the future. The promotion signifies to the employee that he has done a good job and that management is pleased with him and his work. It also signifies to management that its choice in hiring and giving this employee responsibility was a good choice. Management is now saying that it expects even more from the employee. The promotion is both a "Well done" for past work and a challenge for increased work to be done in the future.

TIPS

- Be warm and enthusiastic.
- Be positive about the challenge in the new job to be done.
- Be personal.

Sample 117. Congratulations on a Promotion I

ABC COMPANY, INC.
123 MAIN STREET
CENTERVILLE, IL 66666

March 15, 19XX

XXX XXXXXX XX XXXXXXXXXX
XXXXXXXXXXX
XX XXXXXXX XXX
XXXXXXXXX XX XXXXX

Dear Mr. XXXXXXXXX:

On behalf of the Board of Directors, I am very pleased to inform you of your promotion to Vice President, International Relations.

You have done such a superb job in handling our Asian accounts and in keeping us informed about industry developments in Japan and China that we reached the conclusion that "the world is your oyster!"

You are to start on this new assignment on April 15. As we see it, you have three immediate chores: (1) between now and April 15, get Ted Mills primed to take over the Asian slot as of April 15; (2) learn all you can about the African, Latin American, and European situations as fast as you can, concentrating on Europe first; and (3) prepare for the July exhibition in Frankfurt. You will head our Frankfurt delegation—and you know that the Germans will be showing some mind-boggling new equipment that we will have to better if we want to stay ahead.

Congratulations, Tom. You deserve this promotion. And you have my full support in undertaking the tasks ahead.

Sincerely,

John P. Rogers
President

amc

Sample 118. Congratulations on a Promotion II

ABC COMPANY, INC.
123 MAIN STREET
CENTERVILLE, IL 66666

March 15, 19XX

XXX XXXXXX XX XXXXXXXXXX
XXXXXXXXXXX
XX XXXXXXX XXX
XXXXXXXXX XX XXXXX

Dear Mr. XXXXXXXXXX:

My heartiest congratulations! You've been selected to start up our new line of health books, with the title of Executive Editor, Health Books.

This appointment becomes effective April 15, 19XX, and the starting salary is $_____. Your new office will be on the fifth floor. Please see Jerry Mitchell in Personnel about securing an editorial assistant. As you know, our policy is to advertise these positions in-house before looking outside, so please see Jerry before the end of this week.

We believe that there is a large untapped market for "health books with a difference." Part of your job will be to examine the books in the field and find out what that "difference" is—and then to develop the authors to write to meet that need. Your fine work in developing new books in the general list gives us every confidence that you will enable us to become a leader in this health field also.

Again, my congratulations. And my best wishes as you begin this important new assignment.

Sincerely,

John P. Rogers
President

amc

CONDOLENCE OR SYMPATHY

Employees or members of their immediate family become ill, are injured, or die. Formal dealing with matters such as insurance, leave, and the like, can be handled in a second round of correspondence and telephone calls, often by the person's immediate supervisor or the personnel office. An immediate short and sincere note of support, condolence, or sympathy gives the employee a sense of being cared about, of belonging. Not only is such a letter much appreciated, but it often serves to provide real strength in helping the employee face the crisis.

TIPS

- Send the letter as soon as possible after you learn about the situation. The longer you delay, the less impact the letter will have.
- Be brief.
- Do not become too emotional, yet show real feeling.
- Avoid saying "It's for the best" or other such moralizing platitudes.
- Avoid saying "I know how you must feel," since each crisis situation is unique and the person believes no one else really knows what it is like.

Sample 119. Condolence or Sympathy I

ABC COMPANY, INC.
123 MAIN STREET
CENTERVILLE, IL 66666

March 15, 19XX

XXX XXXXXX XX XXXXXXXXXX
XXXXXXXXXXX
XX XXXXXXX XXX
XXXXXXXXX XX XXXXX

Dear XXXXXX:

I was so sorry to hear that Julia was injured in a car accident over the weekend.

We have no report on the seriousness of the injuries, only that she was taken to a nearby hospital for treatment and observation. I know how much a teenage daughter means to parents, and trust all is not too serious with Julia.

Rachel Bernstein in Personnel will be getting in touch with you next week to help you with the various insurance forms and whatnot.

You, Mary, and Julia are much in our thoughts. Keep us informed as the situation unfolds. Do let me know if there is any way we can be of help in the days ahead.

Sincerely,

John P. Rogers
President

amc

Sample 120. Condolence or Sympathy II

ABC COMPANY, INC.
123 MAIN STREET
CENTERVILLE, IL 66666

March 15, 19XX

XXX XXXXXX XX XXXXXXXXX
XXXXXXXXXXX
XX XXXXXXX XXX
XXXXXXXXX XX XXXXX

Dear XXXXXX:

I was saddened to learn of the death of your mother over this past weekend.

I know there will be many arrangements to make in the days just ahead. If there is anything we can do to make these few days a little easier, please let me know.

Jack will be covering your work, so don't give the job a thought until after the funeral.

Please convey our condolences to your family.

Sincerely,

John P. Rogers
President

amc

THANKS FOR AN EMPLOYEE SUGGESTION

Every company *says* that it welcomes suggestions from employees. A box for such suggestions might be placed in a convenient location; monetary awards might be made for suggestions that are used; and notice of suggestions that have been used might be listed in company newsletters or placed on the bulletin boards. These are means of encouraging the submission of useful suggestions.

Another way of showing you really want—and value—employee suggestions is to send a letter of appreciation when you receive a suggestion. The employee will be quick to tell fellow workers about the letter. Be sure to send a letter of thanks for a suggestion you don't use as well as for those that you do.

TIPS

- Cite the suggestion specifically.
- If you are using—or plan to use—the suggestion, say so and invite future suggestions.
- Praise the employee for showing interest and initiative.

Sample 121. Thanks for an Employee Suggestion (Adopted)

ABC COMPANY, INC.
123 MAIN STREET
CENTERVILLE, IL 66666

March 15, 19XX

XXX XXXXXX XX XXXXXXXXXX
XXXXXXXXXXX
XX XXXXXXX XXX
XXXXXXXXX XX XXXXX

Dear Mr. XXXXXXXXXX:

Thank you for submitting your splendid suggestion that our next edition of word processing software include the feature of cursoring backward and forward by word, by sentence, by paragraph, and by page—as well as by character and line, as we do at present. As you so thoughtfully point out, this feature would enable a user to cursor around in a document much faster and easier than he can at present.

Our Development Group looked into this suggestion and agrees with you. The development of this feature will not only make our word processing program easier to use, but it will also give us a valuable feature to advertise. It will help make our program more competitive.

Please keep thinking about our products with an eye to improvement. Keep those suggestions coming in. It is because we have employees such as you—people who care—that we have made such strides in the past four years.

A copy of this letter will be placed in your personnel file as a formal record of our appreciation. And I am pleased to tell you that your year—end bonus has just grown by $750 for this suggestion.

Again, our thanks.

Sincerely,

John P. Rogers
President

amc

Sample 122. *Thanks for an Employee Suggestion (Not Adopted)*

ABC COMPANY, INC.
123 MAIN STREET
CENTERVILLE, IL 66666

March 15, 19XX

XXX XXXXXX XX XXXXXXXXXX
XXXXXXXXXXX
XX XXXXXXX XXX
XXXXXXXXX XX XXXXX

Dear Mr. XXXXXXXXXX:

Thank you for submitting your excellent suggestion that our next edition of word processing software include the feature of cursoring backward and forward by word, by sentence, by paragraph, and by page—as well as by character and line, as we do at present. As you so thoughtfully point out, this feature would enable a user to cursor around in a document much faster and easier than he can at present.

Our Development Group looked into this suggestion and agrees with you about the desirability of the feature. However, the implementation of such a feature would require a reconfiguration of our keyboard—a development we are not able to implement at this time.

Your suggestion will be kept in the pending file for reconsideration at a time when we open the possibility of redesigning our keyboard.

A copy of this letter will be placed in your personnel file as a formal record of our appreciation.

Please accept this letter also as my personal thanks for your loyalty and commitment to the company. And keep the suggestions coming in!

Sincerely,

John P. Rogers
President

amc

NEW COMPANY DIRECTION

When a company undertakes a new venture, employees wonder how this will affect their job. To allay anxiety, to generate enthusiasm and support for the change, and to quell rumors, a letter that explains what the direction is and what it will mean to the company is a good morale builder. Even though most of the employees were not part of the decision-making process, they deeply appreciate being told what is happening to their company. This kind of letter reinforces their feeling that the company is *their* company. They *want* to feel an integral part of the company—the environment in which they spend so many hours each week—and this kind of letter tells them that the company's management really does believe that they *are* an integral part of the company.

TIPS

- Take pleasure in making the announcement. This new venture is a step forward, not a retreat or retrenchment.
- If certain departments will be affected more than others, note this. It will help those people as they go about putting the changes into practice.
- Thank everyone for helping to make the company a successful one.

Sample 123. New Company Direction I

ABC COMPANY, INC.
123 MAIN STREET
CENTERVILLE, IL 66666

March 15, 19XX

XXX XXXXXX XX XXXXXXXXXX
XXXXXXXXXXX
XX XXXXXXX XXX
XXXXXXXXX XX XXXXX

Dear Mr. XXXXXXXXX:

After months of planning and preparation, I am pleased to announce the creation of a new division in our company. It is the Professional Educator's Computer-assisted Support System (PECASS).

As you know, we have pioneered in the development of "vertical" software programs—programs designed to assist specific professional groups perform highly specific tasks. Our company mission has been, as it continues to be, to serve the professional person with programs that are better than any other available.

The "Professional Educator" is the school district superintendent; the individual school principal; the federal, state, county, or city school administrator; the university dean; and the teacher in a university school of education. Our new PECASS is designed to help the professional educator do the job better, faster, and more accurately. By providing needed information and analyses in a timely fashion, PECASS can aid in making better decisions. Our goal is to place PECASS in every school in the country!

Robert Smith is heading this new company venture. I know you will give him and his staff all the support you have given every project head during the busy days of start—up. Before long, we will all think of PECASS as a part of the company that's been around "forever." But right now, it is a promising baby that needs lots of tender, loving care to start growing.

Thanks for your commitment to our company's growth and for your support for this exciting new program.

Sincerely,

John P. Rogers
President

amc

Sample 124. New Company Direction II

ABC COMPANY, INC.
123 MAIN STREET
CENTERVILLE, IL 66666

March 15, 19XX

XXX XXXXXX XX XXXXXXXXXX
XXXXXXXXXXX
XX XXXXXXX XXX
XXXXXXXXX XX XXXXX

Dear Mr. XXXXXXXXXX:

Our company has made the finest, longest—lasting, most popular Western wear for more than a century. And we will continue to do so with no lessening of our trusted quality.

One of the facts of life, however, is that the number of people who buy our traditional product is diminishing. We have, therefore, established a new division to design and craft sport, play, and work wear for a newer, more fashion-conscious market. We are launching this division on April 1.

You will see the impact of this division in three ways:

1. A new series of TV and magazine ads, highlighting the new look. The "old" look will continue to be promoted in those geographic and demographic areas where it is strong.
2. New fabrics and designs to be manufactured. We will all have to learn new tricks to keep our quality standards intact while working on unfamiliar fabrics and designs. I know we can do it.
3. An upswing for the company that will benefit us all. All-out commitment to making this new venture work is the best way we can all work together to keep our company and our jobs during these days of rapid fashion change. Up until now, we have been fortunate in being exempt from the stress and uncertainties of regular fashion change. Now it is "the name of the game."

If you hear some commentator mention that this development is a "desperation" measure, don't you believe it! Our tomorrow is bright, and with your continued skill and enthusiasm, it will be brighter than ever before.

Sincerely,

John P. Rogers
President

amc

COMPANY REORGANIZATION

Every company will realign its structure from time to time. Employees may see these changes as a threat. A letter that outlines the nature of the change, gives a sound reason for it, and reassures the work force is a sound morale builder.

Company turmoil feeds on misinformation and lack of information. The reasons for a reorganization and the nature of that reorganization are seldom understood or explained positively, so a good deal of uncertainty gets generated by company change. One of your most important communications tasks is to allay employee insecurity by a timely and adequate announcement of important reorganizational changes.

TIPS

- Be brief. If you try to explain too much, you only raise questions that you do not answer in your letter. This can generate more anxiety than not writing the letter at all.
- Be positive. Don't blame someone or some department for having failed in their job.
- Thank everyone for helping to implement the change.

Sample 125. Company Reorganization I

ABC COMPANY, INC.
123 MAIN STREET
CENTERVILLE, IL 66666

March 15, 19XX

XXX XXXXXX XX XXXXXXXXXX
XXXXXXXXXX
XX XXXXXXX XXX
XXXXXXXXX XX XXXXX

Dear Mr. XXXXXXXXXX:

Just as a person has to learn new skills to do more complex work, so a company sometimes has to find new ways of doing things as the work load grows. It's a nice kind of problem to have!

In order to handle our rapidly growing number of franchises and accounts with better service and quicker response, we are reorganizing our regional sales force, effective April 1, 19XX. We are dividing the nation into four Marketing Regions: Eastern, Southern, Central, and Western. Each region will have a Regional Manager: Margaret Olson (Eastern), Harry Baines (Southern), Rolf Johanssen (Central), and Barry Jones (Western). Rolf and Barry are new to the company; Margaret and Harry have been with us for the past two years. The sales force will be increased. Each salesperson on the sales force will be assigned to work in a region under the direction of the Regional Manager. These assignments will be made during the next two weeks.

To coordinate the entire national sales effort, Mark Vinson will be our National Sales Manager. The four Regional Managers will report directly to him, and he reports to me. There may be a little confusion at first, especially in dealing with new regional code numbers in our order and billing processes that will reflect this reorganization.

The last thing we want to do is cause our accounts any trouble or delay while they get used to dealing with new people or new account numbers and procedures. Please handle their orders or queries in any way you can right away, and then fit the paperwork into the new structure on our time—not on their time! By July all the kinks should be worked out throughout our system, and we'll all think of the four regions as the normal way of doing business.

Thanks in advance for your support and cooperation in putting this development into effect. I am confident that the end result will be well worth the effort as will be seen in the greater sales we will have during the months ahead.

Sincerely,

John P. Rogers
President

amc

Sample 126. Company Reorganization II

ABC COMPANY, INC.
123 Main Street
Centerville, IL 66666

March 15, 19XX

XXX XXXXXX XX XXXXXXXXXX
XXXXXXXXXXX
XX XXXXXXX XXX
XXXXXXXXX XX XXXXX

Dear Mr. XXXXXXXXXX:

Organization is a description of who does what to enable a company to do its business. Reorganization is a change—minor or major in nature—of who does what.

Reorganization comes about because of growth, of new ventures, and of different people available to do the work who have special skills and talents. Reorganization is a good sign that a company is adjusting itself to do its job better—and there is always room for improvement.

As of April 1, 19XX, I am setting up a Special Executive Group. This group will meet weekly and will consider major policy matters and concern itself with long-range planning. The group consists of myself (Chief Executive Officer), Tom Bradmont (Chief Operating Officer), and Will Fish (Chief Financial Officer). The group, as such, will not issue orders or have executive authority; it serves as a senior sounding board for myself and the Board of Directors in thinking through future strategy for the company.

From time to time, the group may call for a special study to be done. Such a study will be assigned to one of the group members, who may delegate it to people in his division.

The future in this fast-changing decade is a challenge. We as a company intend to meet the challenge on our terms, not be at its beck and call.

Sincerely,

John P. Rogers
President

amc

INCREASED BENEFITS

When a company adds to its employee benefits, a letter announcing these benefits is a splendid opportunity to enhance goodwill within the company. It is important that the benefit be a real one that the employee can readily perceive.

TIPS

- Express your pleasure at being able to announce the benefit.
- Be specific about what the benefit is.
- Make it clear that the employees have earned the benefit through productive work for the company.
- Express your hope that continued company growth can mean continued additions to the benefit package.

Sample 127. Increased Benefits I

ABC COMPANY, INC.
123 MAIN STREET
CENTERVILLE, IL 66666

March 15, 19XX

XXX XXXXXX XX XXXXXXXXXX
XXXXXXXXXXX
XX XXXXXXX XXX
XXXXXXXXX XX XXXXX

Dear Mr. XXXXXXXXXX:

I am always endeavoring to extend the benefits it is possible for our company to provide its employees.

Since both spouses in so many families now work, the insurance industry has modified its approach to group insurance coverage. Up until now medical insurance has been issued to one working spouse as a family policy; the other spouse "lost" the benefit of medical insurance.

We have just negotiated a group program with our insurer to provide insurance—a wide variety in kinds of insurance—worth a certain amount for each employee; the amounts are based in part on the annual salary. Under the terms of our policy this amount covers major medical benefits, plus a certain amount of life insurance. If it is possible for your medical insurance to be covered by your spouse's policy (whether the spouse works for our company or elsewhere), you can now redirect the value of what your medical premium would have cost the company and use that premium value to obtain some other kind of insurance coverage.

In effect, this benefit gives those of you who previously would have "lost" either your or your spouse's medical coverage benefit the opportunity of securing other kinds of insurance coverage in place of that "lost" benefit.

The personnel office is ready to assist you in looking through the options so you and your spouse can decide what best meets your needs.

We appreciate your loyalty and efforts for the company, and trust you will accept this as another way we can say "Thank you."

Sincerely,

John P. Rogers
President

amc

Sample 128. Increased Benefits II

ABC COMPANY, INC.
123 MAIN STREET
CENTERVILLE, IL 66666

March 15, 19XX

XXX XXXXXX XX XXXXXXXXXX
XXXXXXXXXXX
XX XXXXXXX XXX
XXXXXXXXX XX XXXXX

Dear Mr. XXXXXXXXX:

I am pleased to announce a new employee benefit that has been approved by the Board of Directors.

We are building a Health Center for employee use. The Health Center will be located just up the street at 129 Main Street, in easy walking distance. This

will make it readily accessible for use before or after work, or during the
lunch hour.

There will be locker rooms, a check-in counter for personal valuables, a
swimming pool, a workout room with Triton equipment, an indoor oval track for
jogging and serious running, a sauna, and a steam room.

Employees will have free use of the Health Center facilities. The center will be
open five evenings a week until 9 p.m., including Friday and Saturday.
Employees' children age eleven and older can use the facilities on Friday
evening and Saturday afternoon and evening without cost when accompanied by a
company-employed parent.

We expect the Health Center to be in operation by September 30 this year. As the
day draws closer, you will receive a complete information kit on the center and
its operation.

We hope you will use and enjoy these facilities. They are being provided partly
in response to the recommendations of the Employees Council, whose advice and
suggestions are always so supportive and helpful.

Thank you for your loyal and unstinting work. Your efforts have made the Health
Center possible.

Sincerely,

John P. Rogers
President

amc

CHAPTER 11

Letters to the Media

From time to time you may wish to write a letter to a newspaper, a magazine, or a television station regarding some issue. The issue may deal with a general matter of public concern or a matter that deals more directly with your company.

Your letter may be to correct some statement made about your company by the medium concerned. Or it may be part of your public relations effort to shape public opinion about an issue that directly affects your business.

A letter to the media should be brief, clear, firm, and reasonable. If it is a letter of protest, the protest should be grounded in reason, not emotion. Be sure to have one or two others in the company read the letter over before you send it. Someone else may sense a level of emotional intensity that you would miss because you are too close to the letter and the issue.

CORRECTING MISSTATEMENTS ABOUT YOUR COMPANY

Although you basically believe in the fairness and the accuracy of reporting in the media, you also have probably read or heard reports of events or situations about which you have detailed knowledge. And you know how far short of complete accuracy such a report has been.

It is almost inevitable that you will be dissatisfied in some way with a report about your company that appears in a newspaper, magazine, or on TV. Even so careful a newspaper as the *New York Times* has a standing section in a prominent location for corrections of reports that appeared in earlier issues. If you decide the issue is of such importance to you that you cannot overlook it, you should write a letter to the editor or station manager setting forth your corrections.

TIPS

- Try to keep the letter to one page.
- Be specific in your corrections.
- Offer to provide further substantiation if it is desired.
- Keep your emotions under control.
- Have someone read over your letter, checking for accuracy and tone.

Sample 129. Correcting Misstatements About Your Company I

ABC COMPANY, INC.
123 MAIN STREET
CENTERVILLE, IL 66666

March 15, 19XX

XXX XXXXXX XX XXXXXXXXXX
XXXXXXXXXXX
XX XXXXXXX XXX
XXXXXXXX XX XXXXX

Dear Mr. XXXXXXXXXX:

In the March 12, 19XX, edition of the <u>Herald</u>, it was reported in the financial
section on page C23 that the ABC Company is facing a serious problem in
introducing its new Logical Organizer software, and that this problem may cause
ABC to retrench even to the extent of reducing its work force.

This report is inaccurate and misleading. The report, we fear, may have the
effect of causing some people to think twice about securing ABC software.

1. The Logical Organizer is ABC's entry into the field of idea management and
   organization. The reviews of the program that appear in trade journals
   have made it abundantly clear that Logical Organizer is the most versatile
   and the easiest-to-use such program on the market.
2. Even though our major advertising campaign has just been launched, sales
   of Logical Organizer exceed by three times the projected volume we
   anticipated by March 1. Every indication—from actual sales volume to store
   enthusiasm to user excitement—shows the program to be an outstanding
   success. And this before the promotional campaign is in full swing.
3. Far from reducing our work force, we have only this week determined to
   <u>increase</u> our staff by 3 percent.

For the sake of fairness and media responsibility, we insist that a correction
to your report be printed in the next issue of the <u>Herald</u>.

We would also be pleased to have your reporter visit us at any time so we can
provide him with the facts about the Logical Organizer and ABC. How he
interprets those facts is, of course, his job—but we want him to work from a
factual base, not a rumor base.

Sincerely,

John P. Rogers
President

amc

Sample 130. *Correcting Misstatements About Your Company II*

ABC COMPANY, INC.
123 MAIN STREET
CENTERVILLE, IL 66666

March 15, 19XX

XXX XXXXXX XX XXXXXXXXXX
XXXXXXXXXXX
XX XXXXXXX XXX
XXXXXXXXX XX XXXXX

Dear Mr. XXXXXXXXXX:

In a prime-time news program last night, Steven Morris reported on the situation at the toxic waste site north of Centerville. He implied in his report that the ABC Company (1) was a major polluter at the site with carcenogenic chemicals and (2) was remiss in taking steps to comply with EPA standards.

Our switchboard has not been quiet since.

Steven Morris is in error on both implications. In all fairness, I appeal to you to see that these errors are corrected in an editorial this week on the same news program—and on other news slots where the Morris tape was run.

1. <u>None</u> of the chemicals used now—or ever used—by ABC are carcenogenic in nature. We came into business several years after the Love Canal case broke, and we have been utterly insistent from the beginning that our diskette manufacturing process only use materials that the EPA has certified noncarcenogenic. We have not used "not yet proved" chemicals, as do some of our competitors; we have accepted only tested, proven benign supplies.
2. We have consulted with the EPA and the state Environmental Quality Agency from the beginning of our business to ensure that <u>every</u> rule, regulation, and recommendation regarding the safeguarding of the environment was both understood and followed by our staff. We have voluminous correspondence in our files from these agencies attesting to our cooperation and adherence to their requirements and suggestions. Even though some of their nonbinding suggestions have cost us significantly, we have gladly spent the amounts, for we care deeply about our community as a responsible business should.

We look forward to hearing an updated report with corrections of the misinformation that Mr. Morris broadcast last night. We would be happy to meet with any of your reporters on this subject at any time. We are also writing on this matter to the <u>Herald</u>, since the subject is of such public interest and we feel we have been unfairly treated in your report.

Sincerely,

John P. Rogers
President

amc

SUPPORTING A POSITION

If a news report or editorial comment presents information or an opinion that you wish to support, a short letter giving that support will be most appreciated by the medium. More people will write a letter of criticism than will write a letter of commendation; therefore, your letter of support will be particularly welcome.

Your letter may be printed or reported on, so write it with as much care as you would write a letter correcting misstatements.

TIPS

- Be brief.
- Be specific in your comments about your support.
- Have someone in your office read the letter before you mail it.

Sample 131. Supporting a Position I

ABC COMPANY, INC.
123 MAIN STREET
CENTERVILLE, IL 66666

March 15, 19XX

XXX XXXXXX XX XXXXXXXXXX
XXXXXXXXXXX
XX XXXXXXX XXX
XXXXXXXXX XX XXXXX

Dear Mr. XXXXXXXXXX:

I read with considerable interest your comments in the March 14 editorial on the handling of toxic wastes at the Centerville Waste Disposal Site.

We at the ABC Company fully support your position that only wastes that the EPA has <u>certified</u> as "noncarcenogenic" be disposed of at the site. This position rules out the disposal of wastes about which no certification as yet has been made. There have been too many instances over the past decade in which a substance of uncertain nature was permitted to be disposed of in a community waste site and the substance was only later discovered to be carcenogenic.

From the beginning of our company in 19XX, we have used only certified noncarcenogenic materials in our products. We made this decision as a deliberate environmental choice, even though this has caused significant extra cost in some instances. We did so because we take our community responsibility very seriously. Indeed, our own children and grandchildren are Centervillians.

We commend you for bringing this position so strongly to the attention of our entire community.

Sincerely,

John P. Rogers
President

amc

Sample 132. Supporting a Position II

ABC COMPANY, INC.
123 MAIN STREET
CENTERVILLE, IL 66666

March 15, 19XX

XXX XXXXXX XX XXXXXXXXXX
XXXXXXXXXXX
XX XXXXXXX XXX
XXXXXXXXX XX XXXXX

Dear Mr. XXXXXXXXXX:

In your March 13 editorial on the "Six O'Clock News" you endorsed making a historical district of Main Street from Central Avenue west to Armory Road. You cited several excellent reasons for recommending this step.

We at ABC Company fully support your position. We recognize that we are located in the heart of one of Mid-America's last surviving clusters of manufacturing plants that were constructed during the industrial boom that took place during and right after the Civil War. From our own experience we have found it no more costly to remodel the interior of our old, solid building than it would have been to raze the building and construct a new but far less substantial modern building. We love the feeling that comes for developing twenty-first-century technology in a fine old building that was an integral part of the mid-nineteenth-century technological revolution. Just being in the building gives us a sense of perspective that we would otherwise miss.

We hope to see the Main Street Historical District as a reality within the next six months. And we believe that a moratorium should immediately be imposed on any demolition of standing buildings until the districting question is settled. We are confident that creating a historical district would attract fine businesses to Centerville—businesses that take pride in the community of which they are a part.

Sincerely,

John P. Rogers
President

amc

DEMANDING A RETRACTION

Sometimes a report will be so erroneous that a retraction is the only way to rectify the misinformation. A letter asking for a retraction should be firm but polite. It should deal only with matters of fact.

TIPS

- Be brief.
- Be very specific about what is in error and what you want retracted.
- Expect the medium to make the retraction as a matter of principle.

Sample 133. Demanding a Retraction I

ABC COMPANY, INC.
123 MAIN STREET
CENTERVILLE, IL 66666

March 15, 19XX

XXX XXXXXX XX XXXXXXXXXX
XXXXXXXXXXX
XX XXXXXXX XXX
XXXXXXXXX XX XXXXX

Dear Mr. XXXXXXXXXX:

A report on page C25 of your March 14 issue of the Herald erroneously identified the Chairman of the Board of ABC Company as C. Harold Brown. This report indicated that Mr. Brown is currently under investigation by the state attorney general's office for "insider" stock trading.

The Chairman of the Board of ABC Company is C. Howard Browning, not C. Harold Brown. Mr. Browning is a respected industrial pioneer in microelectronics whose integrity is unquestioned by his colleagues and associates. Your erroneous report has done a great disservice to Mr. Browning and to ABC Company. There is no association at all between ABC and C. Harold Brown.

Please print a retraction of your report in tomorrow's issue of the <u>Herald.</u>

Sincerely,

John P. Rogers
President

amc

Sample 134. Demanding a Retraction II

ABC COMPANY, INC.
123 MAIN STREET
CENTERVILLE, IL 66666

March 15, 19XX

XXX XXXXXX XX XXXXXXXXX
XXXXXXXXXXX
XX XXXXXXX XXX
XXXXXXXXX XX XXXXX

Dear Mr. XXXXXXXXXX:

On your news program last night you reported that the ABC Company was among the leading Centerville businesses that opposed designating a section of Main Street as a historical district.

Your report has greatly disturbed us, since we have been one of the most outspoken <u>proponents</u> of the creation of a historical district. In fact, it was C. Harold Browning, Chairman of the Board of the ABC Company, who sponsored the motion to create the district.

We expect a retraction on tomorrow's news program.

Sincerely,

John P. Rogers
President

amc

CHAPTER 12

Financial Letters

Every business deals with banks, leasing companies, insurance companies, and similar financial institutions on matters of finance. These letters tend to follow standard formulas more than ordinary business letters. The reason this is so is to ensure precision in mutual understanding and agreement about a most important aspect of business life—finances. But even so, the formulas are far less stilted than in earlier days.

BANKING LETTERS

Letters to banks deal with requests for funds, directions about handling accounts and checks, acceptance of proposals or loans, and financial references. As you come to know your banker more personally in the course of your business dealings, your letter can reflect this personal relationship. Any documents you sign with the bank will, of course, be formal and legal.

TIPS

- Be direct, clear, and to the point.
- Make sure that the letter does not mislead or confuse.
- Be brief without being curt.

Sample 135. Banking Letters I

ABC COMPANY, INC.
123 MAIN STREET
CENTERVILLE, IL 66666

March 15, 19XX

XXX XXXXXX XX XXXXXXXXX
XXXXXXXXXXX
XX XXXXXXX XXX
XXXXXXXXX XX XXXXX

Dear Mr. XXXXXXXXX:

This is to confirm our telephone conversation regarding the payoff amount of our outstanding $10,000 ninety-day note.

The note is due on March 27, 19XX. The principle with interest amounts to $10,483.72 if the note is paid by the end of the business day on the twenty-seventh. Each succeeding day calls for an additional $3.83 interest per day. It is our intention, as we discussed, to pay the note on the twenty—seventh.

I have appreciated the arrangements for the note, and I look forward to further business with you in the future as we require such financing.

Let me just add a personal observation. Your teller staff is terrific. Their courtesy, quickness, and overall professionalism shows careful training and good management.

Sincerely,

John P. Rogers
President

amc

Sample 136. Banking Letters II

ABC COMPANY, INC.
123 MAIN STREET
CENTERVILLE, IL 66666

March 15, 19XX

XXX XXXXXX XX XXXXXXXXX
XXXXXXXXXXX
XX XXXXXXX XXX
XXXXXXXXX XX XXXXX

Dear Mr. XXXXXXXXX:

As I discussed with you last week, we have finally decided to expand our operation by purchasing the Bridge Road property. We require commercial mortgage financing in the amount of $248,500 for a twenty—year fixed—interest mortgage. You indicated that the interest rate during the month of March for such a mortgage is ____%, and our board has approved applying for the mortgage at this rate.

I am enclosing the following papers:

       a. Completed mortgage application.
       b. Copy of purchase and sales agreement.
       c. Copy of board resolution and borrowing authority.
       d. ABC Company, Inc., financial statements for 19XX—XX.
       e. Property and property development description.

Since we want to close on this property in early May, your early appraisal of the property and commitment to the mortgage would be most appreciated. May I hear from you next Monday on this?

We have found our banking arrangements with you to be very satisfactory over the past five years. We look forward to moving ahead on this new venture as well.

Sincerely,

John P. Rogers
President

amc

CREDIT BUREAUS

Most of the letters you write to a credit bureau will be inquiries about the credit standing of a potential customer. Credit bureau reports give a history of credit payment promptness as reported by various firms with whom the potential customer has accounts. The credit bureau itself does not make a recommendation about granting credit to the customer.

Very occasionally, you may need to write to a credit bureau to ask about the recording of your own credit history with a view to correcting erroneous information that may have been entered.

TIPS

- Be brief and impersonal but not curt.
- If you think the credit bureau has made a mistake in your case, deal with the matter factually and unemotionally.

Sample 137. Credit Bureaus I

ABC COMPANY, INC.
123 MAIN STREET
CENTERVILLE, IL 66666

March 15, 19XX

XXX XXXXXX XX XXXXXXXXXX
XXXXXXXXXXX
XX XXXXXXX XXX
XXXXXXXXX XX XXXXX

Dear Mr. XXXXXXXXXX:

We are considering a business relationship with the XYZ Corporation of 321 Bridge Road, Centerville, Illinois 66666. The arrangements could involve our carrying an account at times of $50,000.

In order to come to a decision about this account, we would appreciate receiving a confidential credit profile on XYZ Corporation.

Thank you for your help in this matter.

Sincerely,

Herbert H. Harris
Credit Manager

HHH:rd

Sample 138. Credit Bureaus II

ABC COMPANY, INC.
123 MAIN STREET
CENTERVILLE, IL 66666

March 15, 19XX

XXX XXXXXX XX XXXXXXXXX
XXXXXXXXXXX
XX XXXXXXX XXX
XXXXXXXXX XX XXXXX

Dear Mr. XXXXXXXXXX:

In making a routine credit check on our company, our bank came up with a disconcerting piece of information.

They report that you have in your records an indication that we have a 120-day overdue account with the XYZ Corporation of Centerville.

This is not correct. We are—and have been—completely up to date with XYZ Corporation on a regular 30-day basis for the past twelve months. Enclosed are photocopies of XYZ's statements and our canceled checks for the past six months as substantiation of our current status with them.

Please correct your records accordingly and send us a copy of our updated credit report.

Thank you for your prompt help in this matter.

Sincerely,

Herbert H. Harris
Credit Manager

HHH:rd

FINANCIAL INSTITUTIONS

There are other financial institutions besides banks with which companies conduct business. The same principles apply to letters written to these institutions as apply to banks: Be specific, factual, and moderately personal.

TIPS

- Be brief.
- Be specific about the business under discussion.
- Do not be overly formal.

Sample 139. Financial Institutions I

ABC COMPANY, INC.
123 MAIN STREET
CENTERVILLE, IL 66666

March 15, 19XX

XXX XXXXXX XX XXXXXXXXXX
XXXXXXXXXXX
XX XXXXXXX XXX
XXXXXXXXX XX XXXXX

Dear Mr. XXXXXXXXXX:

This is to confirm our telephone conversation of yesterday in which we discussed the leasing of an MNO photocopy machine. You indicated that since we already lease equipment from you, there is no need to fill out an application form. You wanted the model and serial numbers, cost, and firm from whom we are leasing the equipment.

Please prepare the lease documents for:

        MNO Photocopy Machine Model G-0034/32/A
        Serial number: 4285/67/826Z
        Cost: $2,449.50
        Company: Midwest Equipment Company
                765 Elm Street
                Centerville, IL 66666
        Term of Lease: 36 months with buy-out option

Thank you for both the satisfaction of the services you have rendered us during the past five years and for your prompt attention to this new lease.

Sincerely,

John P. Rogers
President

amc

Sample 140. Financial Institutions II

ABC COMPANY, INC.
123 MAIN STREET
CENTERVILLE, IL 66666

March 15, 19XX

XXX XXXXXX XX XXXXXXXXXX
XXXXXXXXXXX
XX XXXXXX XXX
XXXXXXXX XX XXXXX

Dear Mr. XXXXXXXXX:

Enclosed are the following medical insurance forms:

1. Termination of coverage (effective March 1, 19XX)
    Harold B. Smith
    Mary L. Hopkins
    Gloria DeLorenzo

2. Commence coverage (effective March 1, 19XX)
    Joan Vinson
    Robert P. Watson
    Maruta Schmidt

3. Claims
    Sean Regan
    Peter Peterson

Thank you for handling these matters. Your early attention to the claims will be much appreciated.

Sincerely,

Peter Peterson
Comptroller

PP/cnm

TO CREDITORS OR DEBTORS

Sometimes you have to write to firms to which you owe money with some explanation of why payments might be delayed. And sometimes you have to write to people who owe your firm money with explanations about the nature of the debt.

In a letter to a creditor you need to explain enough to keep the business relationship on a steady course and still deal with the problem you have. It is important to keep a creditor informed lest he become unnecessarily concerned about your ability or intent to make payment.

In a letter to a debtor, your primary aim is to get payment. You need to give the debtor the information he needs.

TIPS

- Be brief.
- Be specific about amounts due, dates, and other business information.
- Mention when you expect to make payment or receive payment.
- Be courteous. You do business with the people now and hope to continue doing so.
- Give enough information or explanation but without extensive detail. Generally, people want to know you are on top of the situation; they don't want to know all about the problems that created the situation.

Sample 141. To Creditors or Debtors I

ABC COMPANY, INC.
123 MAIN STREET
CENTERVILLE, IL 66666

March 15, 19XX

XXX XXXXXX XX XXXXXXXXX
XXXXXXXXXXX
XX XXXXXXX XXX
XXXXXXXXX XX XXXXX

Dear Mr. XXXXXXXXXX:

The winter months have been unusually slow for us. We had anticipated several contracts that, regrettably, did not come into being as soon as we had hoped.

We are pleased, however, to report that some of these contracts have been signed and that work is proceeding on the projects. We expect a presently awkward cash flow situation to change for the better within six weeks.

In the meantime, we are making partial payments on our regular accounts. We enclose $_____ toward our account.

We expect to be fully current with you by the end of next month. We are grateful for your understanding and patience during this period.

Sincerely,

Peter Peterson
Comptroller

PP/cnm

Sample 142. To Creditors or Debtors II

ABC COMPANY, INC.
123 MAIN STREET
CENTERVILLE, IL 66666

March 15, 19XX

XXX XXXXXX XX XXXXXXXXXX
XXXXXXXXXXX
XX XXXXXXX XXX
XXXXXXXXX XX XXXXX

Dear Mr. XXXXXXXXXX:

The quarterly allocation of utilities for the second floor of 659 Walnut Avenue are as follows:

October	Electricity	$146.83
	Gas	43.89
November	Electricity	198.78
	Gas	47.31
December	Electricity	172.06
	Gas	39.52
	Total	$648.39

This allocation is based on your owing 68 percent of the bills rendered against the second—floor meter. Photocopies of the bills are enclosed for your records.

This payment is overdue now—since we have been late in sending you this statement. If you are unable to pay in ten days, please let me know.

Sincerely,

Peter Peterson
Comptroller

PP/cnm

CHAPTER 13

Letters About Services and Products

Every company needs to buy products. These range from small quantities of office supplies to large quantities of raw materials for manufacture. And every company requires services. These range from legal and accounting services to maintenance needs to consultants.

Letters dealing with the purchase of goods and services need to be very specific. Actual quantities to the unit, model or serial numbers, trade names, dates, and any other specifications need to be exact. The vendor cannot guess what you want. If later it becomes necessary to return some of the goods or even to dispute the nature of the service or the kinds or quantities of goods provided, you must have detailed and accurate specifications in your letter and/or purchase order in order to substantiate your side of the dispute.

You also need to be specific when asking for bids from several vendors. This is the only way you can be sure of "comparing apples with apples" when the estimates are submitted.

Leaving some information out can create just as much trouble for you as putting in erroneous information. The vendor has to guess at what is not specified. In dealing with bids different vendors may guess differently on the missing specification. This invalidates the reliability of the estimates you receive from them.

You may write to secure a quicker completion date than the one you have originally set. In such a letter you need to win the cooperation of your vendor. You can only succeed in real emergencies, since a vendor will tire of your always pushing him.

All letters to vendors should be courteous. Just because you buy goods or services does not give you license to run roughshod over a vendor. A vendor who is poorly treated will soon find a reason to seek business arrangements elsewhere, no matter how valuable you think your account is to him.

ASKING FOR INFORMATION

You read about goods and services in the newspaper, in trade journals, and in direct mail advertising. You hear about them from conversations and programs. You see something that interests you at an exhibit or at some other company's premises. However you find out, you want to know more.

You should be as specific as you can—granted you are asking for information—to enable the vendor to tell you what you want to know.

TIPS

- Be as clear as you can about the nature of the information you want.
- Indicate that this letter is only to ask for information; you should not promise an order.
- Give a date by which you need information, if appropriate.

Sample 143. Asking for Information I

ABC COMPANY, INC.
123 MAIN STREET
CENTERVILLE, IL 66666

March 15, 19XX

XXX XXXXXX XX XXXXXXXXXX
XXXXXXXXXXX
XX XXXXXXX XXX
XXXXXXXXX XX XXXXX

Dear Mr. XXXXXXXXXX:

We provide editorial and production services for book publishers. Most of our work is done on MNO word processors or MNO personal computers with the Professional WP word processing software.

We normally encode the final copy with generic typesetting codes and communicate the book to a typesetter for final photocomposition.

Please send me information about your Page Organizer software. I need to know how it works on MNO equipment, what it costs, and most importantly, what it will do for us. I am particularly interested in how the hyphenation/justification program works with a variety of composition systems. I realize that one vendor's font is not identical to the same font from a different vendor. How does your system handle the problems that can arise from our use of several suppliers with no uniformity of vendor equipment?

If you have solved these problems, I would welcome a demonstration.

We have several major projects coming in next month. I would appreciate this information by the end of this month, before we start work on these new projects.

Sincerely,

John P. Rogers
President

amc

Sample 144. Asking for Information II

ABC COMPANY, INC.
123 M<small>AIN</small> S<small>TREET</small>
C<small>ENTERVILLE</small>, IL 66666

March 15, 19XX

XXX XXXXXX XX XXXXXXXXXX
XXXXXXXXXXX
XX XXXXXXX XXX
XXXXXXXXX XX XXXXX

Dear Mr. XXXXXXXXXX:

When I attended the INFOMATIC Trade Exhibit in New Orleans last month, I was quite taken with your line of photocopiers with collation and stapling capability.

Please send me a catalog and descriptive literature. I also need to know prices.

I am looking into similar equipment that is manufactured by other companies. There is no need to send a representative to call on us until I narrow the field from a comparison study of features and costs.

This information will be very helpful.

With thanks,

Sincerely,

John P. Rogers
President

amc

ASKING FOR BIDS OR ESTIMATES

Once you have two or more vendors in mind for goods or services, and once you have determined your specifications for work to be performed or goods provided, you are ready to send a letter asking for an estimate. A request for quotation is a standard method of informing yourself of what a vendor will charge. Since considerable work may go into preparing a response to your request for quotation, do not send one out unless you are reasonably serious about using the vendor.

Even if you initially secure an estimate by telephone or in a personal conversation, it is good business practice to have it confirmed in writing. Having the estimate on paper means that both purchaser and vendor can discuss the same job in the same terms, with minimum chance for confusion or misunderstanding.

TIPS

- Be clear about what you are asking for. Specify quantities, serial and model numbers, dates, and any special requirements.
- Ask for a reply in writing.
- If there is a schedule that must be met, make it very clear that the schedule is an integral part of the request.

Sample 146. Asking for Bids or Estimates I

ABC COMPANY, INC.
123 MAIN STREET
CENTERVILLE, IL 66666

February 17, 19XX

XXX XXXXXX XX XXXXXXXXXX
XXXXXXXXXXX
XX XXXXXXX XXX
XXXXXXXXX XX XXXXX

Dear Mr. XXXXXXXXXX:

Please give me an estimate for the printing and binding of 250 copies of the large management manual. A copy of this manual is enclosed for the purpose of the estimate. If we proceed with the order, use this copy of the manual for direct same-size reproduction purposes, using Inlox paper plates.

Specifications:

Paper	60# offset white
Color	One color (black)
Cover	10-pt. light blue Carolina Board
Cover color	1-0-0-0 (black)
Binding	GBC
Printing	Two sides of each sheet
Trim	8½" x 11"
Packing	Shrink-wrap each manual, pack 25 manuals per carton

The job is to be completed no later than May 3, 19XX and delivered to us on or before May 8, 19XX.

Please let me have your estimate for the job by March 25.

We have appreciated the work you have done for us in the past and look forward to a continuing relationship of mutual benefit.

Thanks,

Sincerely,

John P. Rogers
President

Sample 146. Asking for Bids or Estimates II

ABC COMPANY, INC.
123 Main Street
Centerville, IL 66666

March 15, 19XX

XXX XXXXXX XX XXXXXXXXXX
XXXXXXXXXXX
XX XXXXXXX XXX
XXXXXXXXX XX XXXXX

Dear Mr. XXXXXXXXXX:

Our medical insurance coverage is up for renewal at the end of June. Because of the competitive and changing nature of the health insurance field, we are considering bids from three or four companies for our coverage. We would like to consider an estimate from your company.

I am enclosing a copy of our present contract. You will note the nature of the coverage and the people (and their ages) who are covered by our present policy. There is no change in the personnel to be covered.

We desire at least the same levels of coverage. If you are able to provide greater benefits at little or no additional cost, we will, of course, listen very carefully to you.

We need to make a presentation to our Board of Directors about our coverage at an April 28th meeting. We would appreciate having a bid from you no later than April 21, in order to give us time to prepare this information for the board's consideration.

We would be happy to consult with one of your representatives to clarify our needs on your benefits, but we need the bid in writing for formal consideration.

Thank you for your help in this matter.

Sincerely,

John P. Rogers
President

amc

PLACING AN ORDER

When you have considered a bid from one or more vendors and have decided to place the order, you should confirm the order in writing (even though the order may have been given by telephone). Here again, the letter should contain all the specifics. This letter can be considered a legal contract even though it may not be phrased in contractual language.

TIPS

- Be specific about what you are ordering.
- If you need the goods or service by a specific date, make this clear in your order.
- Express your pleasure in placing the order.

Sample 147. Placing an Order I

ABC COMPANY, INC.
123 MAIN STREET
CENTERVILLE, IL 66666

March 15, 19XX

XXX XXXXXX XX XXXXXXXXXX
XXXXXXXXXXX
XX XXXXXXX XXX
XXXXXXXXX XX XXXXX

Dear Mr. XXXXXXXXXX:

Thank you for your letter of March 10, 19XX, with your estimate of $_____ for printing, binding, packing, and delivering 250 copies of the large management manual according to the specifications outlined in my February 17th letter.

I am pleased to place the order with you. Please use the copy of the manual that we sent to you for estimate purposes as camera-ready copy.

May I remind you that we must have these manuals delivered on or before May 8, 19XX. We are using them at that time in a seminar for new middle management appointees.

Thank you for your continued splendid service.

Sincerely,

John P. Rogers
President

amc

Sample 148. Placing an Order II

ABC COMPANY, INC.
123 MAIN STREET
CENTERVILLE, IL 66666

March 15, 19XX

XXX XXXXXX XX XXXXXXXXXX
XXXXXXXXXXX
XX XXXXXXX XXX
XXXXXXXXX XX XXXXX

Dear Mr. XXXXXXXXXX:

This is to place an order for three (3) folding tables and two (2) secretarial posture chairs. These items are shown in your 19XX catalog as follows:

Page	Item	Description	Price
149	K357Y	Beige Folding Table	$ 57.50
297	M964S	Red Secretarial Posture Chairs	174.95

Please deliver these items to our warehouse at 765 Commerce Drive, Centerville, but bill us at our main office at 123 Main Street, Centerville.

If you are unable to deliver these items by April 25, 19XX, please call Mr. Johnson at (309) 123-4567.

Thank you for your prompt attention to this matter.

Sincerely,

John P. Rogers
President

amc

REJECTING A BID

When you find it necessary to reject a bid, do so as soon as possible. The vendor has hopes that he will receive the order. Even though he tells himself not to count on business until the order is in hand, he still may hope. It is a courtesy to let him know in a timely way that he will not be getting the order. This courtesy is especially appreciated by a small business, one in which every order counts.

If you think it would be helpful to tell the vendor why you have rejected the bid, do so briefly and thoughtfully. Such a comment may help the vendor to decide whether to adjust future bids.

TIPS

- Thank the bidder for the bid and assure him that you have considered it carefully.
- Explain why the bid was not accepted if you think an explanation would be appreciated by the vendor.
- Tell the vendor that you hope you can do business in the future.
- There is no need to tell this vendor where you placed the job.

Sample 149. Rejecting a Bid I

ABC COMPANY, INC.
123 MAIN STREET
CENTERVILLE, IL 66666

March 15, 19XX

XXX XXXXXX XX XXXXXXXXXX
XXXXXXXXXXX
XX XXXXXXX XXX
XXXXXXXXX XX XXXXX

Dear Mr. XXXXXXXXXX:

Thank you for your estimate on our medical insurance coverage for the year beginning June 1, 19XX.

Our Board of Directors carefully considered your proposal, along with those of four other companies. The final decision was between you and one other company. On the combined cost/benefit basis, we have decided to accept the other company's proposal.

Thank you for your complete submission and explanation in depth of the benefits under your policy. We shall be reviewing our coverage again in two years.

With all good wishes, I am

Sincerely,

John P. Rogers
President

amc

Sample 150. Rejecting a Bid II

ABC COMPANY, INC.
123 MAIN STREET
CENTERVILLE, IL 66666

March 15, 19XX

XXX XXXXXX XX XXXXXXXXX
XXXXXXXXXXX
XX XXXXXXX XXX
XXXXXXXXX XX XXXXX

Dear Mr. XXXXXXXXXX:

Thank you for the estimate of $_____ for printing, binding, packaging, and delivering 250 copies of our large management manual.

Regretfully, we have decided to place the order elsewhere. The primary reason for this decision is not based on the quality of your work; we have always been very pleased with your work. The reason is based on price. Your bid came in 20 percent higher than the next closest estimate.

We shall be continuing to place printing jobs—both new work and reprints—and will continue to invite your quotations on this work.

With all good wishes,

Sincerely,

John P. Rogers
President

amc

LETTER OF COMPLAINT

Not every service or product meets your satisfaction. When you are dissatisfied, you should voice your dissatisfaction. One reason for doing so is to help the vendor know there is a problem. The problem may have been created at a lower level in the vendor's company, and the vendor himself may not know about it. You render him a service when you bring weaknesses or failures to his attention.

A second reason for writing a letter of complaint to a vendor is to seek redress. You may not wish to pursue the matter so far as to take legal action, but you may wish to give the vendor the opportunity of making good. Most vendors value your business and their reputation sufficiently to replace defective goods, resupply work that did not meet specifications, or refund money when necessary. No vendor *likes* to do so, but your carefully worded letter of complaint may motivate him to do so.

TIPS

- Be courteous though firm. You will not win a vendor's cooperation by anger.
- Be reasonable. Show logically and factually that the fault lies with the vendor or his claims. The vendor should be impressed with your fairness and quiet grasp of the facts in the matter.
- Be specific about what is wrong. Be equally specific about what you want done about it.
- Tell how you have been hurt or inconvenienced by the problem. This strengthens your argument for redress.

Sample 151. Letter of Complaint I

ABC COMPANY, INC.
123 MAIN STREET
CENTERVILLE, IL 66666

May 15, 19XX

XXX XXXXXX XX XXXXXXXXXX
XXXXXXXXXXX
XX XXXXXXX XXX
XXXXXXXXX XX XXXXX

Dear Mr. XXXXXXXXXX:

The shipment of 250 large management manuals that we ordered on March 15, 19XX, for delivery on May 8, 19XX, did not arrive until May 14. When they did arrive, the ink on the covers was still not dry, and therefore, the covers smudged when handled. A sample is enclosed to show the appearance of the manual after a single day's use in our seminar.

This job is not at all satisfactory to us.

1. The late delivery is inexcusable, since we made it very clear when we wanted the manuals in hand and why. Our seminar leaders and students worked under a serious handicap without the manuals in hand.
2. The smudging suggests that the job was done at the last minute, without allowing prudent time for the ink to dry before shrink—wrapping. The appearance of the manual does not meet our professional expectations; you equally should be professionally distressed to have this work advertised as yours.

We request that you reprint the job at no cost to us, so we can replace the manuals that were distributed at the seminar. We expect this new printing to be in our hands by June 15, 19XX. Please call Mr. Robbins at Extension 163 if this request presents any problem to you.

Thank you for your cooperation on this matter.

Sincerely,

John P. Rogers
President

amc

Sample 152. *Letter of Complaint II*

ABC COMPANY, INC.
123 Main Street
Centerville, IL 66666

March 15, 19XX

XXX XXXXXX XX XXXXXXXXX
XXXXXXXXXXX
XX XXXXXXX XXX
XXXXXXXXX XX XXXXX

Dear Mr. XXXXXXXXXX:

During the past year we purchased three (3) MNO word processing systems with the Model 1110-1 letter quality printers. We use these systems to prepare highly technical manuals and books, using the LQP printouts as camera-ready copy. We purchased MNO equipment on the basis of company sales representatives' assurance—backed up by company brochures and manuals—that the LQP could print with two printwheels (roman and italic) with perfect alignment.

The systems have not performed according to those claims since the first day we used them. We have called in your service engineers to try to fix them; we have discussed the matter with numerous regional and headquarters technical advisers. We have records of some eighty-five hours of service time spent on the systems trying to make them perform to advertised standards.

In the meantime, our work has suffered enormously. We have had to go to extra expense to send work out to be done on other manufacturer's systems in order to appear right. We have had enough expense and inconvenience.

We require a full refund for all the equipment on the grounds that your company has misrepresented its performance capabilities. Please have someone call me at the beginning of next week about that matter; we can make arrangements then for pickup to return the systems to your warehouse.

I look forward to hearing from you on this matter in the immediate future.

Sincerely,

John P. Rogers
President

amc

LETTER OF COMPLIMENT

Vendors generally receive more letters of complaint than of compliment. People tend to make the effort to write when they are angry or want redress more than when they are pleased and satisfied. It is a good business practice to send a letter of compliment to a vendor when the vendor has gone to some extra trouble to serve you or has manufactured a product that exceeds your expectations.

This is an easy letter to write. The greatest difficulty you face in writing such a letter is just taking the moment in a busy day to do so. A letter of compliment, however, is worth its weight in platinum as an ambassador of goodwill for your company.

TIPS

- Be brief but generous in your comments.
- Be specific about products, situations, and people.
- Express your pleasure in the vendor's goods or services and your anticipation of continuing to use them.

Sample 153. Letter of Compliment

ABC COMPANY, INC.
123 MAIN STREET
CENTERVILLE, IL 66666

March 15, 19XX

XXX XXXXXX XX XXXXXXXXX
XXXXXXXXXXX
XX XXXXXXX XXX
XXXXXXXXX XX XXXXX

Dear Mr. XXXXXXXXX:

We have five MNO word processing systems and two MNO personal computers. Our business requires having all this equipment on line and at work.

Last week we had a massive power failure during a freak afternoon thunderstorm. Although we have surge-protection devices, the impact of the electrical company's switching efforts to handle community power needs proved too much. The systems crashed and we faced a tight deadline for work in process.

We put in an emergency call for service. Our regular service engineer, Tom Readman, was overwhelmed with calls, but nevertheless he called to make arrangements to arrive at 10:45 p.m. Tom worked on the equipment until well past 2 a.m. When our staff came in that next morning, the systems were all up and running. We made our deadlines!

Your company prides itself on first-class equipment and superb support. Our experience says that you have every right to that pride.

Be assured that MNO will supply our future computer equipment needs.

Sincerely,

John P. Rogers
President

amc

CHAPTER 14

Letters About Employment

There are two kinds of letters you may write about your own employment situation. One is a letter seeking employment; the other is a letter of resignation.

Every person wonders at some time whether the grass is truly greener in another field. Indeed, it often is. It is not unusual for a person to change jobs in the same general field two or three times in the course of a career. It is becoming more common for a person even to change fields in the course of a lifetime.

Letters often play a critical role in asking about a new job possibility, in seeking an interview, or in exploring new areas of work—geographically or vocationally.

SEEKING EMPLOYMENT

Since it is usually wise not to let your present employer know you are job hunting, your letters of inquiry should be sent as a confidential letter. Responses should be sent to your home address, unless you want the office grapevine to spread the word that you are looking for a job elsewhere.

Rather than send out scores of identical letters, which of necessity are "canned" in nature, send out a letter that is very specifically addressed to an individual company. Put yourself in the place of a personnel director or CEO of a small company. Wouldn't you be more responsive to a letter that addressed you by name and that spoke quite thoughtfully of how the person could serve the needs of your company in some knowledgeable, specific way? It only takes a little research to be able to speak in concrete terms about the company to which you are writing.

Make it clear that you are seeking more than just more money. You are seeking opportunity for career development; you are seeking the chance of linking your future with this particular company that you hold in high regard; you are looking for the chance to contribute to the fortunes of this company. Your letter inquiring about employment is in essence a sales letter: You are selling yourself.

Don't tell everything there is to tell about yourself. Tell only what you think will be of enough interest to the person to whom you are writing to make him want to meet you. Tell only those matters that have relevance to the company you are writing to.

If you enclose a résumé, do not send a "stock" résumé. Edit the information in a full résumé, so that the résumé you send includes basically information that shows how you can help that company. Focus your résumé just as much as you focus your letter.

TIPS

- Write to a particular person by name. If you need to, call to find out who to write to, and get the correct title.
- Tell what you can do for his company. This presumes you have learned what his company does best or needs most.

- Write about your strengths.
- Tell the person you will call in a week concerning an appointment. This shows you have initiative, but that you also prepare the ground.
- If you are from out of town, explain when you can travel for an interview.

Sample 154. Seeking Employment I

876 Peachtree Lane
Atlanta, GA 33333
March 15, 19XX

John P. Rogers, President
ABC Company, Inc.
123 Main Street
Centerville, IL 66666

Dear Mr. Rogers:

At the INFOMATIC Convention I heard that you are looking for sales representatives as part of your growing position in the market.

For the past three years I have been the sales representative for FGH Incorporated, working in the southeastern states from Virginia to Louisiana. I have tripled the number of accounts during that period and have increased the dollar volume of sales five times since I started in the territory.

Since I know the FGH product line thoroughly, I have often wished I had in my bag some of the ABC line. With your programs, your support of your programs at the customer level, and your national promotion of your line, I could have more than doubled the sales growth I did have. Now I hear there is a chance to sell your line and participate in the growth of the industry's leading innovator.

I would be pleased to visit Centerville during the last half of April to discuss this possibility. I enjoy the Southeast and have a wide range of contacts here that could be very profitable for ABC. However, I do want you to know that I am not "wedded" to working in the Southeast.

May I call you next week to confirm a date?

Looking forward to carrying this conversation on to the next step, I am

Yours sincerely,

Martin R. Robinson

Sample 155. Seeking Employment II

876 Beech Road
Centerville, IL 66666
March 15, 19XX

<u>CONFIDENTIAL</u>

John P. Rogers, President
ABC Company, Inc.
123 Main Street
Centerville, IL 66666

Dear Mr. Rogers:

This is in response to your advertisement in the <u>Herald</u> for a comptroller.

For the past four years I have been the assistant treasurer at LMN Limited here in Centerville, and prior to that I was head bookkeeper for a department store in Chicago. As assistant treasurer, I oversee the day-to-day functioning of both the bookkeeping and accounting departments, as well as prepare the long-range forecasts for management. I participate in management planning committees, so I have a good grasp of both the practical and the strategic features of a comptroller's responsibility.

I have an accounting degree from the Illinois Institute of Technology, and I have completed most of my MBA from Indiana University on an extension basis. This is an indication of my commitment to be thoroughly professional in this field.

I would welcome the opportunity of discussing this position with you and to indicate more personally what I can contribute to ABC. May I call you next week to determine the most convenient time for such a discussion?

Sincerely yours,

Alan L. Parsons

REQUEST FOR LETTER OF REFERENCE

You may wish to ask for a letter of reference about someone you have an interest in hiring. Your request should indicate the general area in which you plan to use the person and ask for an assessment of skills and experience in that field. You may also want to have a general character reference.

TIPS

- State that this is a confidential letter of request for a reference.
- Give the addressee some idea of the field of interest that you have, so he can write to your question.

- Offer to reciprocate.
- Thank him for his help.

Sample 156. Request for Letter of Reference I

ABC COMPANY, INC.
123 MAIN STREET
CENTERVILLE, IL 66666

March 15, 19XX

XXX XXXXXX XX XXXXXXXXX
XXXXXXXXXXX
XX XXXXXXX XXX
XXXXXXXXX XX XXXXX

Dear Mr. XXXXXXXXXX:

Martin Robinson of FGH Incorporated has given me your name as a reference. He is seeking employment with us and we are sufficiently interested to seek further information.

Mr. Robinson has applied for a sales representative position. It involves considerable travel to service present accounts and to open new accounts. It includes training the accounts to handle our software product line with understanding and to inspire them to handle the line with enthusiasm. The job involves a great deal of "self-starter" traits.

Any assessment you can give about Mr. Robinson along these lines would be much appreciated. We would appreciate your holding this inquiry in confidence for the present time, since we do not wish to cause him any unnecessary problems in his present circumstances.

If I can be of any help to you in the future, please let me know.

Many thanks.

Sincerely yours,

John P. Rogers
President

amc

Sample 157. Request for Letter of Reference II

ABC COMPANY, INC.
123 MAIN STREET
CENTERVILLE, IL 66666

March 15, 19XX

XXX XXXXXX XX XXXXXXXXXX
XXXXXXXXXXX
XX XXXXXXX XXX
XXXXXXXXX XX XXXXX

Dear Mr. XXXXXXXXXX:

Alan L. Parsons has applied to us for the position of comptroller.

He has indicated that he once worked for you as head bookkeeper. We would be very grateful for any comments you may wish to make about Alan's work and fiduciary trust that might aid us in making a decision about his application.

The position of comptroller at ABC includes general oversight of both bookkeeping and accounting functions, contributing to the financial aspects of our corporate long-range planning, management of our investment and pension portfolios, and serving as the principle financial advisor to the Board of Directors.

We would appreciate your keeping this request in confidence at the present time, and we assure you that your response will also be held in strict confidence.

If I can reciprocate at any time, please let me know.

Sincerely,

John P. Rogers
President

amc

LETTER OF REFERENCE

You must be careful in writing a letter of reference not to include any information that could later be used against you in a legal suit or that would embarrass you if you met the person about whom you wrote. There are "sunshine" laws that enable a person to see his personnel file. Your letter of reference would normally be a part of that file.

Speak positively about the person as you have knowledge of him. Speak about the experience and skills of the person in the pertinent field of interest, if that has been mentioned. Give a general character reference. If you wish to be negative about the person, do it with indirection, such as, "We feel that marketing is not his strongest suit, even though he has tried very hard to improve."

TIPS

- Be brief. The person wants an overall impression, not a detailed "report card."
- Be as positive as you can be.
- "Damn with faint praise" rather than condemn outright, if you feel you must.
- Indicate whether you would be pleased to have the person work for you.

Sample 158. Letter of Reference I

TRU ENTERPRISES
456 WALNUT STREET
ATLANTA, GA 33333

March 25, 19XX

John P. Rogers, President
ABC Company, Inc.
123 Main Street
Centerville, IL 66666

Dear Mr. Rogers:

In your letter of March 15 you ask about Martin R. Robinson, indicating that Martin has applied for a position as a sales representative.

Martin is one of the finest salesmen I have ever seen in operation. He learns his products, he charms his customers, and—most important of all—he knows how to close.

He is one of those people who can be so effective in the field that he faces the danger of being promoted out of his best contribution to a company. Martin's easygoing relationship with his colleagues and sometimes indifferent attitude to excessive paperwork make him a better sales person, for instance, than a sales manager.

If you want to see sales in an area grow significantly, you couldn't make a better choice than Marty Robinson.

Sincerely yours,

Robert E. Leeson
Sales Manager

REL:jl

Sample 159. Letter of Reference II

RST DEPARTMENT STORE
456 LAKE AVENUE
CHICAGO, IL 60000

March 25, 19XX

John P. Rogers, President
ABC Company, Inc.
123 Main Street
Centerville, IL 66666

Dear Mr. Rogers:

This is in response to your inquiry about Alan L. Parsons, who has applied for the post of comptroller in your company.

Mr. Parsons worked for us from 19XX to 19XX, rising to the position of head bookkeeper. He started out as a bookkeeping clerk while he attended IIT part-time. We found his work to be entirely satisfactory and were sorry to lose him when he left to take a job in Centerville that afforded him a better opportunity. He was quite reliable in fiscal matters. We would be pleased to have Mr. Parsons back on our staff.

Although I cannot comment on Mr. Parsons's capabilities on the larger management matters you mentioned since he did not have those responsibilities with us, I remember him as an intelligent, quick, healthily ambitious person who was studying to improve himself.

With hope that this will be of some help to you, I am

Sincerely yours,

Peter K. Remsen
Executive Vice President

PKR/ym

LETTER OF RESIGNATION

When you resign from a position, a short letter of resignation is both courteous and necessary. It completes the record of your employment and states for the record your reason for voluntarily leaving.

If you are leaving in protest or anger, wait a few days before writing the letter. Be clear and honest in your statement, but keep your emotions under control. Don't unnecessarily close the door for future relationship with the people, since you never know under what circumstances you will meet them again. In the "musical chairs" of job changes, you may be surprised who turns up where in the future.

TIPS

- Be brief. This is not the place for a long letter of protest or anger.
- State the reason why you are leaving. Use the reason you want the company to use in public statements. Give them the words to explain why you are leaving.
- Use the phrase "for personal reasons" if indeed the reasons are related to your personal—not professional—life or if you would rather not create conflict by stating your real reasons.
- If you are leaving under pleasant circumstances, express your pleasure in having worked for the company and your respect for your colleagues.

Sample 160. Letter of Resignation I

ABC COMPANY, INC.
123 MAIN STREET
CENTERVILLE, IL 66666

March 15, 19XX

John R. Rogers, President
ABC Company, Inc.
123 Main Street
Centerville, IL 66666

Dear Mr. Rogers:

This is to tender my resignation from the ABC Company, Inc., as comptroller, effective April 15, 19XX.

As you know, my son was seriously injured in an automobile accident last year and suffered severe—and evidently permanent—brain damage that requires an entirely different style of life on the part of Mary and myself than we are able to provide at the present time. We are accordingly moving into a rural environment, establishing a small retail business, and refocusing our priorities in order to care more fully for Bob.

I have enjoyed working for ABC. More importantly, I have appreciated working with you. You have become a good friend as well as a respected boss. I shall miss both the company and the opportunity of developing so many of the projects we have planned together. The comptroller's team has been terrific, particularly in their support and understanding during the past five months.

With a combination of appreciation and sorrow, I remain

Sincerely,

Warren M. Muller
Comptroller

WMM:hdr

Sample 161. Letter of Resignation II

ABC COMPANY, INC.
123 MAIN STREET
CENTERVILLE, IL 66666

March 15, 19XX

John P. Rogers, President
ABC Company, Inc.
123 Main Street
Centerville, IL 66666

Dear Mr. Rogers:

This is to resign from the ABC Company, Inc., as of April 15, 19XX.

It has been evident for some time that the new educational software department
which I established has not had full company support. I can understand this in
terms of the retrenchment brought about by this year's economy, even though I
had hoped any retrenchment would not affect this new venture. I would imagine
that my leaving at this time also resolves a difficult problem of what to do with
me in the light of this general reduction.

I have appreciated the opportunity you gave me. I'm sorry that things for the
department did not work out, for whatever reasons. And I hope to keep in touch
with you and with ABC friends.

I wish you and the company well for the days ahead.

Sincerely,

Timothy Ryan
Director, Educational Software

TR:amw

SEEKING AN EMPLOYEE

Sometime you may wish to initiate a conversation with someone who works elsewhere
about working for your company. You have seen certain job performance or professional
qualities that you desire for your company. A letter to such a person should be a "feeler."
Firm negotiation about job, salary, title, and the like, is for later face-to-face discussion, if he
is interested.

TIPS

- Ask the person if he is interested in opening a conversation about a job with you.
- State one or two circumstances about the job or the company that you think will be of
  interest.

- Ask the person to get in touch with you by letter or telephone. Don't be too eager in pursuing the person lest you create too high expectations.
- Mention a quality in the person or his work that you admire.
- Indicate you are looking forward to a response.

Sample 162. Seeking an Employee I

ABC COMPANY, INC.
123 MAIN STREET
CENTERVILLE, IL 66666

March 15, 19XX

XXX XXXXXX XX XXXXXXXXXX
XXXXXXXXXXX
XX XXXXXXX XXX
XXXXXXXXX XX XXXXX

Dear Mr. XXXXXXXXXX:

We are looking for a proven field sales representative to open up a new territory for us in the Northwest. The territory would include Washington, Oregon, Idaho, Montana, Wyoming, and Nevada. From our perspective, this is virgin country. We have no accounts there and do only minor direct mail sales.

I have seen your work with FGH Incorporated over the past few years and have talked with many salespeople in our field. From what I have seen and learned, you are the person we would like to discuss the job with. We would, of course, provide a combination commission, bonus, and base draw, as well as full expenses in an incentive package that will be of interest to you.

If you are interested in further discussion, please call me collect and we can set up a time to meet.

I look forward to hearing from you soon.

Sincerely,

John P. Rogers
President

amc

CHAPTER 15

Business Letters and Electronic Word Processing

With the widespread availability of electronic word-processing capabilities in today's offices, business letters can be more quickly and accurately produced. The authors have elsewhere written on how to word process *(Word Processing Made Simple)* and how to type on a microcomputer *(Computer Typing Made Simple)*. Rather than develop that information here again, an annotated list of ways in which electronic word processing can be used to enhance the task of business letter writing and production follows. Because each office has a unique structure and its own kinds of word-processing capability, this list is generic and suggestive in nature rather than machine specific and instructional. Each executive and secretary can implement features from the following list in accordance with actual business needs and with the hardware and software in hand.

FORMAT

Set up page format defaults on your program diskette with the settings you want for your letters and memos. These settings should include:

1. Sink (the distance in numbers of lines from the top of the page to the line on which the first line of typing starts; the sink leaves room for the letterhead on the first page of a letter).

2. Left and right margins.

3. Line spacing (single, one-and-a-half, or double); most business letters are single-spaced, with an extra line of space between paragraphs.

4. Page length for first page and for subsequent pages.

5. Headers for pages after the first page (number [2], number with hyphens [-2-], or number with name [Jones - page 2]).

With these defaults set for your standard letter and memo formats, the word processing system automatically does all the formatting work for *every* letter you work on.

SPELLING VERIFICATION

If your system has a spelling verification or "dictionary" feature, use it to check the spelling of each document. Typographical errors can always slip in. Although the spell check feature will not point out properly spelled words that happen to be used incorrectly ("if" instead of "is") or ungrammatically ("they was" instead of "they were"), the feature will unerringly pick up many slips that you might miss in a rapid reading of the letter before signing ("persmission" instead of "permission").

If your system allows you to make your own additions or supplements to the dictionary, make such a supplement of company names, abbreviations, titles, terms, and special terms you use in your business that do not appear in the system's own dictionary. By using this supplement along with the system dictionary, you ensure consistent correctness of spelling for these special company names and terms.

You want your letter to be as accurate and correct as possible, since it conveys to the reader something of the kind of person you are. So use every available electronic aid to make your letter-writing system produce a better product.

"BOILERPLATE" OR STORED PARAGRAPHS

For many of your routine letters, you will eventually settle on standard ways you want to express yourself. These standard paragraphs may be of your own devising, may be taken from *Business Letters Made Simple*, or they may be a combination. Once you have determined how you want these ten or fifteen paragraphs worded, you can number them and place them in the word-processing system for future, continuous use. These stored paragraphs can be called out by number from a diskette and placed into a document. Then they can be reproduced in the letter without change, or they can be changed to have different names, model numbers, prices, dates, and the like, to fit that particular letter.

Use of standard, stored paragraphs saves you from having to reword the same basic paragraph over and over. It enables the electronic system to reproduce the paragraph without error and faster than it would take you to reword it each time you dealt with the subject.

Prepare a folder of your stored paragraphs. Organize the paragraphs by frequency of use and subject matter. Refer to the folder as you do your correspondence, so you can accurately call up the proper paragraph by number. Revise your folder and your paragraphs at least once a year to keep it abreast with the nature of your correspondence and the way you want to express yourself.

LIST PROCESSING

If you want to write the same letter to several people (even several hundred) and you want the letter to be an original, typed letter rather than a printed or photocopied letter, your word processing system will merge a list of names and addresses with the body of the letter to give you automatically typed original, personal letters. The system will also use the list of names and addresses for the envelopes or mailing labels without having to retype them.

This list processing feature can be especially useful in sales letters, in company announcements, in collection letters, or in any situation where you send the same letter to ten or more addresses.

COPY FEATURES

If you send the same letter to two—or even up to about ten—different people, it is easy to use the system's copy feature to produce error-free letters in a minute or two. Make a copy of the first (original) letter. Change only the name and address lines, and print out the letter. Repeat this for the other addresses.

If you want to send the letter to more than about ten people, it is worth the effort to list process the letter.

MATHEMATICAL FEATURES

If your letter has columns of numbers that need to be added, multiplied, subtracted, divided, or any combination, use the math feature in your system to do these calculations and to print out the results. The result will be neater and certainly accurate. Make the system do as much of your work for you as possible.

TABLES AND COLUMNS

If your letter has tables or columns—whether of numbers or words—use your system's table-formatting feature. You can save hours of experimenting with trying to create the right format when you let the system create that format for you automatically.

Once you have formatted a table or column that you use regularly, you can save that format on a diskette for future copying. You don't have to "reinvent" it each time you use it.

REPORTS THAT REPEAT DATA

Some reports made in monthly letters repeat "last month" data as well as include "this month" data. This is often expressed in columns of numbers. You can copy the previous letter's "this month" data into the new letter "last month" column, saving the effort of retyping the entire column. Only the new data needs to be typed in for "this month" information.

FILE COPIES

Because copies of letters kept only on word-processing diskettes are easily subject to damage or loss, we recommend that you photocopy every letter and file the copy in your normal fashion. There are many reasons a letter can vanish if the only copy you have is the one on the diskette:

1. The diskette can be damaged.
2. The diskette can be misplaced (lost).
3. The diskette can be misfiled.
4. The letter can be erased.
5. The "name" of the letter on the diskette can be forgotten and become almost impossible to locate, especially if operators change over a period of time.

By making a hard copy (one on paper) either by printing an extra copy out or by photocopying, you keep a physical record of your correspondence in your files.

DISKETTE MAINTENANCE

Periodically maintain your correspondence diskettes. Erase out-of-date letters. Update stored paragraphs. Update addresses you use regularly for list processing.

If you keep a hard-copy file copy of your correspondence, there is generally no need to keep a letter on a diskette for longer than a month. You can, of course, reuse your diskettes almost without limit.

FREQUENT LETTERS

If you write very often to the same ten or fifteen people, create a separate document for each one, such as the "Jones letter." Enter a complete letter for the first use. Every time after that when you write to Jones, revise the "Jones letter" document: change the date line, type in the new body of the new letter, delete the body of the old letter, and leave the opening and closing data unchanged. This method will save a great deal of time in producing such correspondence.

IMPROVED COMMUNICATIONS

Because you now have the capability of sending personal, list-processed letters to a large group of people with only little more effort than it takes to send a single, original letter, you can keep in closer touch with key people.

A sales manager can write with news and encouragement to his sales force more often and with less effort. A sales person can write to key accounts more often. Company employees can receive company news and reports in a more personal and timely fashion from senior management. Use this facility for easier communications to embark on a program of actually providing better, more frequent communications to key customers, staff, and vendors. Your business will be in better shape because your key people will be more in the know and feel more an integral part of it.